The Kids' Nature Almanac

The Kids' Nature Almanac

Great Outdoor Discoveries and Activities for Parents and Children

Alison Smith

Illustrated by Jennifer Harper

Crown Trade Paperbacks

New York

To Him who maketh all things new again,
And to Connor Warfield Smith

Permission to reprint The Lakota Indian Moon Calendar on page 6 courtesy of Kim Nernberger of The St. Joseph's Indian School at Chamberlain, South Dakota.

Published by Crown Trade Paperbacks, 201 East 50th Street, New York, New York 10022. Member of the Crown Publishing Group.

Random House, Inc. New York, Toronto, London, Sydney, Auckland

CROWN TRADE PAPERBACKS and colophon are trademarks of Crown Publishers, Inc.

Manufactured in the United States of America

Design by Lenny Henderson

Library of Congress Cataloging-in-Publication Data
Smith, Alison.
The kids' nature almanac: great outdoor discoveries and activities for parents and children / written by Alison Smith—1st ed.
          p.   cm.
Includes bibliographical references and index.
1. Natural history—Juvenile literature. 2. Nature study—Activity programs—Juvenile literature.
[1. Natural history. 2. Nature study.] I. Title.
QH48.S63   1995

508—dc20   94-25410
                                                            CIP

ISBN 0-517-88293-0
10 9 8 7 6 5 4 3 2 1
First Edition

Contents

Contents

Contents

Acknowledgments

I would like to thank Clare Costello, Alison Picard, Irene Prokop, and Sharon Squibb for their help on the publishing end of this project.

I also wish to thank the following experts in various fields who read my articles and gave me the benefit of their years of experience. Their kindness in taking on this work on the basis of a phone call or letter from a total stranger is very much appreciated. Any errors in this book are mine. Much of the material came from lifelong contacts with people like those listed below who spent most of their time outdoors, or wishing they were outdoors. That list is a book in itself, and I am forever in their debt.

John Ghiorse, meteorologist, Channel 6, WLNE, Providence, RI

John C. Gibson, Coast Guard officer, Windsor, CT

Bill Gucfa, astronomer, Pawtucket, RI, and Seagrave Observatory

Mr. and Mrs. Don Hazelton, maple orchardists, Dummerston, VT

Paul Horowitz, principal scientist, B.B.N., Cambridge, MA

Mr. and Mrs. George Leslie, Papillon Park, Westford, MA

Joyce Merrill, Little Folks Nursery, Saco, ME

Kim Nernberger, artist and teacher, St. Joseph's Indian School, Chamberlain, SD

David Rodriguez, Thousand Islands Sanctuary, West Kingstown, RI

Tiffany Crockford

A Short But Important Introduction

*T*his is a handbook for parents who would like to spend more time outdoors with their children, and feel more at home out there. It is a book of small pleasures. Nothing explodes (well, there is an exploding pumpkin in February) or races wildly out of control (I forgot about the ice sleds in December) or hovers silently in the night sky, giving everyone the cold chills (oops . . . there is a night kite, in March). This is a book of quiet pleasures (probably not all that quiet, since every project involves children in some way). Let's start over. Consider this handbook to be something like a pupu platter. You'll try a little of this, a little of that, and enjoy it–but eventually you'll decide that you want a lot more of tempura shrimp. To help you pursue your choice of subjects more deeply, to go beyond this handbook, we have included the names of other helpful books and agencies.

Some of the projects may take ten minutes . . . others could be carried on for weeks. We've tried to keep costs down and entertainment value up, so that while the kids are learning, they're having fun. (Also cookies. We are great believers in sweetening the educational process.)

The time you spend looking for white oak acorns or tadpoles will not be wasted, even if you don't find any white oak acorns or tadpoles. To quote a great American story teller, Garrison Keillor, "Nothing you do for children is ever wasted. They seem not to notice us, hovering, averting our eyes, and they seldom offer thanks, but what we do for them is never wasted. We know that as we remember some gift given to us long ago."*

Do not hesitate to take your kids by the hand and tackle the natural world even if science was never your favorite subject and you can't remember what equinox means. If we bring a subject up, we explain it. And to quote another great American, Rachel Carson, "If a child is to keep alive his inborn sense of wonder . . . he needs the companionship of at least one adult who can share it, rediscovering with him the joy, excitement and mystery of the world we live in . . . I sincerely believe that for the child, and for the parent seeking to guide him, it is not half so important to know as to feel."**

*From *Leaving Home,* by Garrison Keillor, published by Viking Penguin, 1987.
** From *The Sense of Wonder,* by Rachel Carson, published by Harper and Row, 1965.

January

Is It True—What They Say About Wolves?

The full moon in January is called the Wolf Moon by some Native American tribes. Other tribes call the December moon "Moon When the Wolves Run Together." Certainly wolves do howl more in the winter, and the sound travels farther in the clear, cold air. Perhaps they are calling the pack together to hunt more often because food is scarce and deep snow makes hunting more difficult. Perhaps howling is part of their courtship ritual. It may be that sometimes they just like to howl. Whatever the reason, there is no sound like a pack of wolves howling to make the hair on your arms stand up.

The wolf has long been the victim of bad press. From early childhood on, we have all heard the myths and fairy tales, and seen the artwork depicting the wolf as a scrounging, drooling, evil-eyed monster with six-inch fangs and about a foot and a half of tongue draped out one corner of his excessively large mouth. He has consistently been portrayed as a sort of shark of the woods . . . death on four feet. Have you ever heard of a werebear? I think not. It's the werewolf, but it's the teddy bear. How about Red Riding Hood and the Big Bad Moose? (Moose aren't as handsome as wolves, and at certain times of the year, male moose can be quite short-

1

tempered.) But no, it's Red, who was a troublemaker from the start and still got all the good lines, and the Big Bad Wolf.

The truth is that if you dump all the fables and fairy tales and take an unbiased look at the real animal, you find a beautiful, intelligent creature with an extraordinary sense of family. All the adult wolves in a pack—not just the pups' parents—display interest in and patience with the pack's pups and defer to them when feeding, as we ourselves might if food were scarce and we wanted to be sure our children got enough. The pups play with the older wolves and seem to demonstrate real affection for them. A whole lot of face-licking goes on. All the adult wolves in the pack appear to feel responsible for the pups and will take turns standing guard or minding them when the rest of the pack goes hunting. (In spite of this loving care, the pup mortality rate is quite high.) The wolf usually mates for life. This is not the kind of behavior we think of when we describe a human as a "wolf."

As a rule, wolves avoid humans whenever possible, but it is not true that no healthy wolf has ever attacked a human being in North America. After all, everything has attacked us at one time or another—cats, dogs, bears, rabbits—and we have taken a swing at everything that swam, ran, or flew past us at one time or another, so why should wolves be different? But attacks on humans by wolves are extremely rare, much rarer, for instance, than attacks by other mammals such as bears. Certainly wolves have done nothing to provoke the kind of treatment they have received from man over the centuries.

Under normal conditions the wolf hunts to survive and feed his family. He brings down the sick, the slow, the weak, and the older members of wild grass-eating herds. In the long run this culling benefits the herds themselves. If food is short (and in the winter on the open range, food is almost always scarce by springtime) only those who are likely to be able to keep the herd going and growing will survive predation to share it.

It is interesting to learn just how successful the wolf is as a predator. Barry Lopez says in his book *Of Wolves and Men* that, of a 160-member group of moose observed traveling through wolf territory, only six were actually brought down. The other moose were ignored, defended themselves successfully, or got away. When you consider the size and power of the average adult moose, the risk to the wolves was considerable.

Talk to the kids about what wolves are really like, and ask them how they would rewrite some of the old fairy tales. For instance, this business of Red Riding Hood . . .

Let's say Red hasn't seen her grandmother in quite a while and wonders how Granny's getting along, so she packs up a little basket of day-old bread and apple juice, and sets off through the snowy woods. She loves visiting Granny, who keeps little silver dishes full of chocolate kisses on every table. A neat little old lady.

On the way, Red runs into a wolf, who is perfectly civil, inquiring after her health and Granny's, and then goes on his way.

When Red gets to Granny's house, no one is home. It is obvious when she gets inside that no one has been home for a while: no chocolate kisses in the silver dishes, no milk in the fridge. Red panics and runs outside. She notices wolf tracks in the snow. She jumps to conclusions and heads for home, telling everyone she meets that the wolves must have gotten Granny.

The wolves are shocked. They wouldn't dream of doing away with Granny, but no one will believe them. On Saturday nights when the wolves get together and jam in the moonlight on a hill outside of town, they take to singing the blues . . . a sad sound that causes strong men to shiver, kind women to weep, and little children to pull the covers over their heads.

What happens next? Concoct your own versions of Red Riding Hood or the Three Little Pigs, as told by the Wolf, or start with a brand-new line: "There was a young wolf, once, who was lonely, and every time there was a full moon he would go to the highest hill around and howl, to see if any other wolf would answer. . . ." The kids can take turns adding a sentence to the story as it goes around the room (lots of silliness and giggling with this method), or one child can make up the story and another illustrate it, or everyone in the family can put in their two cents' worth whenever they think of a good story twist. The possibilities are endless.

ORGANIZATIONS SPECIFICALLY INTERESTED IN PROTECTING WOLVES:

WOLF HAVEN
3111 OFFUT LAKE ROAD
TENINO, WA 98589

HOWL
4600 EMERSON AVENUE S.
MINNEAPOLIS, MN 55409

NORTHERN MICHIGAN
WOLF SANCTUARY
117 CASE STREET
NEGAUNEE, MI 49866

A Moon Calendar for Your Tribe

*J*anuary being the month for breaking in new calendars, maybe your tribe—the Charley Smiths of Madison Street—can make its own moon calendar, using titles that have a special significance for all of you. The kids can consult an almanac for the dates of full moons and identify each one on a big homemade calendar (poster board or newsprint, and Magic Markers) with a title and a drawing in the margin or on the appropriate square.

Our family moon names might be:

JANUARY	THE WOLF MOON
FEBRUARY	THE MOON OF DEEP SNOWS
MARCH	MOON WHEN THE SWAMP SINGS
APRIL	THE NEW LEAF MOON
MAY	MOON WHEN APPLE BLOSSOMS FALL
JUNE	MOON OF TALL GRASS
JULY	THE CORN MOON
AUGUST	THE BLOOD MOON
SEPTEMBER	MOON THAT SEES THE BIRDS LEAVE
OCTOBER	THE PUMPKIN MOON
NOVEMBER	MOON WHEN OAK LEAVES FALL
DECEMBER	MOON OF THE FIRST SNOW

Other tribes have used names such as Moon When Trees Split (in the extreme cold of January or February nights), Moon When Berries Ripen, Hunger Moon. These words instantly convey an image. You are there listening to the tree

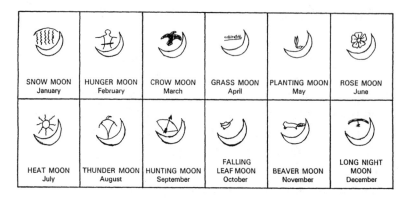

SNOW MOON January	HUNGER MOON February	CROW MOON March	GRASS MOON April	PLANTING MOON May	ROSE MOON June
HEAT MOON July	THUNDER MOON August	HUNTING MOON September	FALLING LEAF MOON October	BEAVER MOON November	LONG NIGHT MOON December

The twelve pictographs above are the ways some Lakota referred to the twelve months of the year.

Pictographs are not the same for every band of Lakota. Some groups used different pictographs for the months or moons of the year.

split—feeling the gnawing in **your stomach,** tasting the berry juice as it spills out over **your lips and** dribbles down your chin.

The kids might get some illustration ideas from this group of pictographs from St. Joseph's Indian School in Chamberlain, South Dakota. They are typical of symbols favored by one branch of the Lakota tribe. A crescent moon was probably used for design's sake; it leaves a very pleasing space for the drawing of the month. You could use a full moon and place your particular pictograph inside the circle of the moon's face.

Talk it over and see what natural event comes to mind with each child when you talk about a certain month. If things get off to a slow start, begin with the season instead. Say, "What do you think of when you say 'spring'?" That should trigger plenty of associations.

Bluebirds: "Young Family Needs Good Home . . ."

You may have heard of the Bluebird of Happiness, but how many bluebirds have you actually seen in the last ten years? Not many, probably.

The bluebird used to be one of this country's favorite birds. It gobbled up harmful insects as if it were paid to do so by the U.S.D.A.; it was one of our loveliest-looking birds; its song was delightfully musical; it was one of the first birds to come north in the spring; and it became quite tame around the yard or farm if encouraged to do so. What more can you ask of a bird?

Unfortunately, the eastern bluebird population has fallen far below what it was at the turn of the century, and the western bluebird is in trouble, too. The main reason seems to be lack of housing, and for that, we are responsible. In 1850 or 1851, depending on your source, someone released a few house, or English, sparrows in Central Park. In 1890 someone else liberated a hundred starlings in Central Park. What was it about Central Park? (Rumor has it that these introductions were part of someone's plan to have every bird mentioned in Shakespeare's work present in the New World. As Will himself might have said, "Who knew?") Neither the sparrow nor the starling was a native bird, but it didn't take these birds long to make themselves at home in all the hollows and cavities our bluebirds had been using for nest sites. Starlings and sparrows are prolific and aggressive birds, but the bluebird is a gentle soul and not much of a fighter. The newcomers have now virtually excluded the bluebird from many of its old territories. And as if that wasn't bad enough, we have land-

7

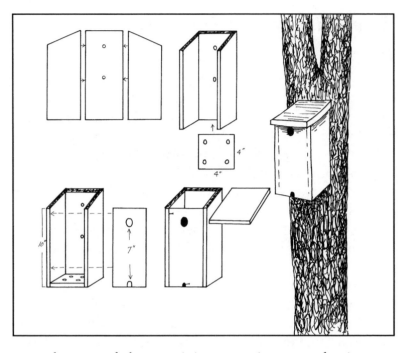

scaped many of the remaining nest sites out of existence. Friendly old apple trees that used to be allowed to decay slowly while small animals and countless families of nestlings grew up in and around them have been cut down and reduced to firewood, leaving a shaven square of sod where once a veritable nursery stood. Wooden fence posts became unpopular. The metal ones lasted longer, were installed more easily, and supported fencing very efficiently. But the old wooden posts supported both board fencing and generations of bird families, deep within their decaying hearts.

Fortunately, there is something that you and I can do to bring the bluebirds back in greater numbers or at least help the survivors maintain their present numbers. We can build bluebird boxes. It's a good idea to make the boxes now, in

January, and put them out as soon as they're finished because the bluebird is one of the first songbirds to arrive from the South, and the boxes will appear more natural if they've had time to weather.

Dimensions for the box itself may vary slightly, but there are several features that may not be changed or overlooked if it is to be successful.

The opening must be 1½ inches in diameter, and no more—so it will keep starlings out but still admit bluebirds. Unfortunately, some sparrows can squeeze through an opening that size. If they do, you may have to narrow it to 1¼ inches wide (sparrows are chubbier than bluebirds) or evict the sparrow as soon as you notice him going in and out with pieces of dry grass in his stout little beak. For this reason and to make cleaning the house once a year easier, it's a good idea to leave the front of the house or the bottom hinged and hooked so you can open it up easily.

Don't attach a perch to the front of the house. Other birds may sit on it and keep the bluebirds at bay until they give up, even if there's no way the intruders can get in there themselves. Experts used to recommend that you place the box between three and five feet above the ground, but most neighborhoods have substantial domestic cat populations nowadays, and mounting a nesting box only three feet aboveground is like presenting the neighborhood cats with a bluebird buffet. Put it at least five feet aboveground. If you attach the box to a post, try to cat-baffle the post with sheet metal rolled around it just below the box or apply a thick coat of petroleum jelly to the post all the way to the ground.

The bluebird is a bird of open spaces. If you put the box on a tree, place it on the open side of the tree where branches and leaves do not come between the box and the fields

THERE IS AN ORGANIZATION, THE NORTH AMERICAN BLUEBIRD SOCIETY, THAT SELLS BLUEBIRD BOXES AND SUPPORTS BLUEBIRD EDUCATION, RESEARCH, AND TRAILS (LINES OF WELL-DESIGNED BOXES MOUNTED IN GOOD BLUEBIRD TERRITORY). YOU MAY CONTACT THE SOCIETY AT P. O. BOX 6295, SILVER SPRING, MD 20916.

beyond. Check a box mounted on a tree at least once a year for secure fastening. A growing tree will sometimes shrug a box off.

Holes drilled in the corners of the bottom will drain off any rainwater that seeps in. Use well-seasoned wood if possible; it won't split or warp. Thick wood—¾ inch to 1 inch—is best, providing better insulation from heat and cold than thin pieces of wood, or plastic or pottery. A slight overhang will protect the entrance from bad weather. A ¼-inch space left between the roof and one wall, or small holes drilled in the sides and front above the level of the opening, will enhance ventilation on the hottest days.

Any well-designed bluebird box should immediately remind you of the type of place bluebirds would select naturally if left to their own devices—a hollowed-out post or the decaying heart of an old apple tree. It will be deep, with an opening high up on one side.

If you make more than one box, place them about one hundred yards apart. Bluebirds won't nest close to other bluebirds. This is probably a built-in natural control to prevent overlapping of feeding ranges. It isn't essential that all your boxes actually be on your property. If another family has a good location and is willing to have you put up a box, go for it. The more boxes there are out there, the greater the odds that your neighborhood will begin to build its own bluebird population.

Ask the kids to help you build the boxes. It is more important to help them feel that they are contributing than it is to get the corners exactly square. Just make sure, before that last nail is driven, that no nails protrude inside the box. We don't want any skewered bluebirds here. It would sort of defeat the purpose of all this.

Paw Prints in the Snow

*I*f you wake up some Saturday morning to find two or three inches of fresh snow on the ground, organize a tracking party. Most suburban or partly rural areas support a thriving hidden community of wild animals. What the Dawn Chorus is to birds (see June), a light, fresh snow is to the animals on your lot: Each reveals the true extent of a population. You will be amazed at the number of unseen four-legged tenants with whom you have been sharing your land. Tracks may change radically or even disappear under the influence of sunlight, so get your group outdoors by mid-morning.

It is fascinating to follow animal tracks, identify them, and speculate on the reasons for their routing. Over here, a mouse came up from underneath the snow to nibble on some wild

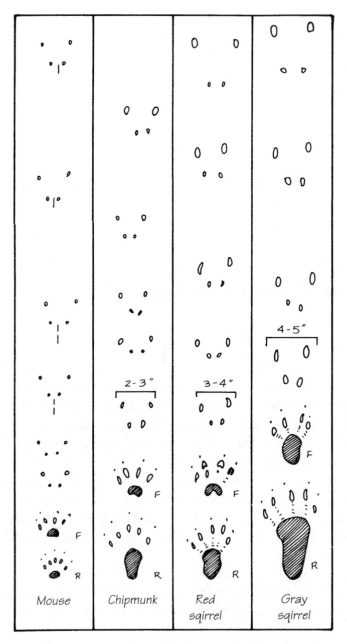

Mouse   Chipmunk   Red sqirrel   Gray sqirrel

January

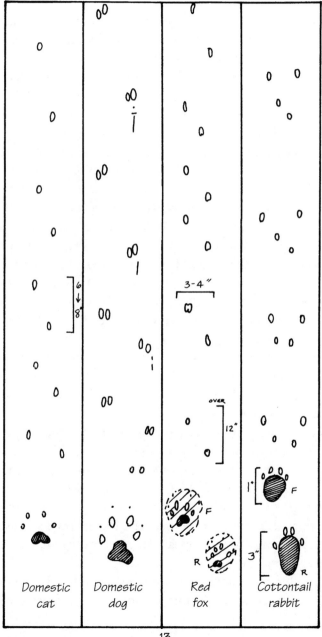

| Domestic cat | Domestic dog | Red fox | Cottontail rabbit |

grass seeds. Once you know where to look, you can trace his little turning, twisting trail under the snow and find the small thicket where he is spending the winter. Over there, several rabbits had dried apple for breakfast. You can see where one rabbit went farther afield, looking for variety in his breakfast perhaps, and where he suddenly stopped, turned, and raced for home in long, bounding tracks. What frightened him? Are there other tracks telling you who was after him? If there are no nearby tracks, he may have been escaping from a hungry hawk. Chances are pretty good that your rabbit made it home. Predators are by no means always successful. If you find evidence that a predator was successful, it may help the kids accept it if you point out that what was death for the prey was life for the predator. At some later time the predator may become someone else's prey. All of nature depends on a closely woven system of checks and balances, on energy being converted from one form to the next. That's what the food chain is all about.

Since you don't want cold or hunger to interfere with your mighty hunters' concentration, a stout breakfast is in order and a pocketful of high-carbohydrate snacks. Think of this as sweetening the learning process.

You are probably already aware of what cat and dog tracks look like. You should also get to know what chipmunk, gray and red squirrel, mouse, cottontail rabbit, and red fox tracks look like. (See pages 12–13.) Depending on where you live, you might even discover deer, moose, or coyote tracks. Remember that the distance between sets of tracks is usually significant: long distances mean flight; short distances, browsing or caution.

Search along the margins of wooded areas, beside creeks, up and down stone walls, around brush piles and dense thickets, and under the bird feeder. You may have fed some early morning visitors who weren't wearing feathers.

For further reading, consult *A Guide to Animal Tracking Behavior* by Donald and Lillian Stokes and, for the delight of the very young, *Winnie the Pooh* by A. A. Milne—the original version, chapter 3, "In Which Pooh and Piglet Go Hunting and Nearly Catch a Woozle."

A Bird in the Hand: Hand-Taming Wild Birds

It is possible to hand-tame wild birds. You don't have to be a Svengali or a Saint Francis to do it. All you have to do is meet one of the bird's basic needs—food—and, during these food transactions, convince the bird that it can trust you. The process does take time—a few minutes every day—patience, and some sensitivity to the bird's reactions, but it is worth it.

Because the hand-tamer must be, above all, calm and patient, this is not a project for the very young child. Older children—from the fourth grade up, say—can handle it and may have the birds eating out of their hands before you do.

You begin the process by producing food for the birds on a regular, dependable basis. They will begin to count on the fact that you will refill their feeder every day. After a month of routine feeding, they will come directly into the feeder moments after you have finished filling it. They're watching the feeder and associating your presence there with getting fed. Eventually there'll be a day when the feeder is empty, the weather is severe, and the birds come into the feeder while you are standing only four or five feet away. It is clear now that they recognize you and trust you to some degree.

Stand a little closer to the feeder every day, after you've filled it, and wait a few minutes. Don't stare at the birds. Look at the ground and relax. Birds seem to feel apprehensive when we look directly at them. They may relate a steady scrutiny to the intense gaze of a predator. Breathe normally, change position when you have to, and think of yourself as just waiting for a bus.

At first, when you are waiting like this a few feet from the feeder, even the bravest bird will let four or five minutes pass before it swoops in, snatches a seed from the tray, and darts away. There may be dozens of aborted missions when it starts to come in and changes its mind inches away from the seed. Eventually, though, it will come in fast, grab a sunflower seed, and depart to a safer perch for eating. All the other birds in the yard will be watching this procedure, and taking notes. It won't be much longer before they start coming in to feed while you are only two feet or so from the seed tray. Remember that twenty-four inches is arm's reach. If you decided to do so, you could grab a bird at that distance, and they know it, so this is real progress.

Next time you go out to fill the tray, stand close to the empty feeder and hold your hand, palm up, loaded with sunflower seeds, as close to the feeder as is comfortable. If the feeder is sturdy, rest your hand on the tray. If you hold your hand too high, it will tire quickly. An alternative position is sitting in a deck chair right beside the feeder with your hand resting on the arm of the chair, palm up. (Put some layers of newspaper on the seat and back of the chair before you sit, to insulate you from the cold.) The advantage of this position is that you can hold it comfortably forever. If you decide to go with the chair, leave it in place all the time so the birds won't have to get over a fear of the chair every day as well.

There will probably be lots of aborted landing attempts before one brave little chickadee actually touches down on your fingertips. He may be so overcome, he won't even remember to get his seed. That's okay. He'll be back. The first time a bird landed on my fingers this year, he came back for his seed in about three minutes, and within the next five minutes, four other birds followed suit. Eventually they will light on your hand almost as soon as you get into position.

A few tips: Try not to swallow noticeably when the birds are coming in close. It makes you look as if you're salivating, and they are likely to assume that your mouth is watering for *them*. Don't worry too much about moving. The birds know that you're not a tree. They know a human being when they see one. The idea is not to disguise yourself, like a hunter in a blind, but to convince them that you can be trusted.

It is all right to let the feeder go empty for an hour or so to create the hunger that will compel the birds to come closer to you than their natural caution would permit, but don't hold out or forget to feed them later whether you make any progress on a given day or not. *Never* let them go into a winter night hungry; some of them might not make it to morning if the weather is severe. Being hungry is uncomfortable for us. Being hungry, even just overnight, can be fatal for a bird whose metabolism is much more rapid than ours. On a winter day the feeder should be stocked at least once by three-thirty in the afternoon so that every bird can fill up before he turns in for the night. Unless your child is exceptionally reliable, it is probably better to have an adult assume the responsibility for filling the feeder.

No matter how patient and gentle you and the older children are at training sessions, no bird will respond if he's chased and yelled at by the younger kids when he comes into the feeder at other times. The exuberant ones are going to have to chase and yell at something else for a while. Each other, perhaps?

I started taming in mid-January, standing three or four feet from the feeder after I had filled it. On March 8 several chickadees took sunflower seeds from my hand while I was sitting in a chair beside the feeder, so the whole process took only seven or eight weeks. There were days when I didn't work on hand-taming at all. There were days when the birds wouldn't come near the feeder, a discouraging thing to have happen after you've invested so much effort, but it probably had more to do with a hawk circling overhead or a neighbor's cat hiding in the nearest hedge than it did with me. Sometimes I put in ten or fifteen minutes at the feeder, most days it was five minutes. On days when the birds took another big step forward, I stayed out there long enough for them to repeat it several times, to reinforce new behavior.

There are differences in shyness between different species, and even between members of the same species. Chickadees seemed to respond more quickly than any other group in our yard. Some species, such as cardinals, did not seem able to come to us at all.

When the courtship season arrives and there are insects for the taking everywhere, you will see a change in feeder behavior. The birds will still come, but they will not be as needy as they were in the winter, and their main interest will be in establishing territory, courting, and raising a family. They will come to your hand much less often. This is natural, a temporary lull.

When a wild bird finally trusts you enough to perch on your finger, you can hardly believe how light and fragile he is, how beautifully and subtly colored. It's hard not to be moved by the experience.

Little Squirrels, Beavers, and Bears

There are days in January when it's hard to believe that the earth has already turned toward spring, but it has, figuratively speaking. The days are getting longer. The last day of January, at the 40th latitude, will be fifty minutes longer than the first, and in snow-covered dens, tree cavities, and underwater lodges, new life is already stirring.

The gray squirrel mates during the months of December, January, and February, and the naked, blind little babies appear forty-four or forty-five days later. They will weigh about half an ounce each. Ask the budding scientist in the group to weigh out half an ounce of something on the postage scale and hand it around. (Our scale is elderly and somewhat infirm, but it tells me that two nickels weigh more than half an ounce and that a tablespoonful of dry rice grains weighs just a little less than half an ounce.) Every fall we watch the mother squirrel in the big apple tree in our backyard gather the best dry grasses and leaves from the lawn and carry them up to her hollowed-out home, preparing a nest for these fragile babies.

The beavers are mating now, too. The little ones will be born in three and a half to four months. The pond may sleep under a foot of solid ice and snow may cover the beaver lodge, but life is going on down there just the same.

Native black bears are dozing the winter away in carefully selected winter dens. The cubs will be born in the dens from mid-January to early February. The babies are blind and almost naked at birth. They weigh just half to three-quarters of a pound and are only six to nine inches long. The kids will understand how very tiny the cubs are if you hand them three sticks of butter (three quarters of a pound) to heft and ask

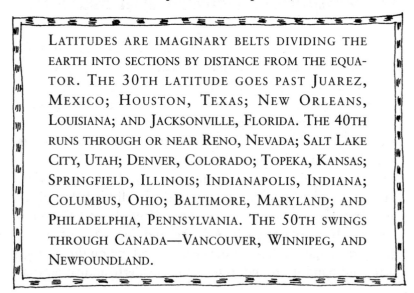

LATITUDES ARE IMAGINARY BELTS DIVIDING THE EARTH INTO SECTIONS BY DISTANCE FROM THE EQUATOR. THE 30TH LATITUDE GOES PAST JUAREZ, MEXICO; HOUSTON, TEXAS; NEW ORLEANS, LOUISIANA; AND JACKSONVILLE, FLORIDA. THE 40TH RUNS THROUGH OR NEAR RENO, NEVADA; SALT LAKE CITY, UTAH; DENVER, COLORADO; TOPEKA, KANSAS; SPRINGFIELD, ILLINOIS; INDIANAPOLIS, INDIANA; COLUMBUS, OHIO; BALTIMORE, MARYLAND; AND PHILADELPHIA, PENNSYLVANIA. THE 50TH SWINGS THROUGH CANADA—VANCOUVER, WINNIPEG, AND NEWFOUNDLAND.

IT CAN TAKE UP TO THIRTY MINUTES FOR YOUR EYES TO ADJUST COMPLETELY TO DARKNESS, BUT FORTUNATELY TOTAL ADJUSTMENT IS NOT NECESSARY FOR YOU TO SEE THE STARS WE DEAL WITH IN THIS BOOK. TURN OFF THE PORCH LIGHTS, ENCOURAGE THE KIDS TO BE PATIENT, AND WATCH THE STARS POP OUT AS YOUR ABILITY TO SEE THEM INCREASES MINUTE BY MINUTE.

them to measure out six to nine inches on a ruler. Adult black bear males are between fifty and seventy inches tall from their paws to the tops of their shoulders and weigh from two hundred to six hundred pounds, which makes the range of size from newborn to fully grown adult greater in bears than in any other mammal except the marsupials. When you're talking about these little bear cubs, tell each child how much he or she weighed at birth and how long he or she was in inches, and mention that the average fully grown adult male in your family weighs—you fill in the blank.

Of course, by the time spring warmth coaxes their mother outdoors, the cubs will have become furry little devils weighing four to five pounds each. While their mother took her winter nap, they nursed and grew rascally.

It's comforting to know that the spring tide of new life is already on the move.

The Great Square of Stars

*T*he Great Square is a good beginner's star project because it is a simple shape created by bright stars in a relatively uncrowded part of the sky. To find it, face due west.* Starting at the horizon and working your way up toward a point directly overhead, look for a big square outlined by four bright stars and tipped up onto one corner. If you're stargazing around seven in the evening, you should find it about halfway up the sky to the zenith (the point directly over your head).

The Great Square is not, technically speaking, a constellation. It is an asterism, which means it is a well-known group that was not one of the original eighty-eight named constellations and so does not qualify as one now. Surprisingly, the Little Dipper and the Big Dipper are also asterisms. Some of the original eighty-eight constellations are less well known and visible than these asterisms, but astronomers must have decided that changing the rules at this point would only result in more confusion.

Pegasus, the winged horse, is right below the Square, and Andromeda, the chained lady, right above it; and stars of the Great Square are part of both constellations. They are much

---

*We will talk about finding due west, north, south, and east in May, and that is an interesting project in itself, but for now, you might invest in a small pocket compass. You can pick one up for about three dollars at the nearest nature store, sporting goods store, or Audubon gift shop. Ask if they carry small compasses that are attached to mini-thermometers or flashlights. These compasses are not much bigger than a dime, but they do the job. The whole unit can be fastened to a zipper pull, a buttonhole, or a key ring. Very handy.

ANYTIME YOU CAN SEE A CONSTELLATION, BUT THE KIDS ARE HAVING TROUBLE DISTINGUISHING IT FROM THE OTHER GROUPS OF STARS UP THERE, TRY USING A FLASHLIGHT AS A POINTER. IF THERE IS ENOUGH WATER VAPOR IN THE LOW-LEVEL AIR FROM MELTING SNOW OR DAMP SOIL, YOUR FLASHLIGHT BEAM WILL GLOW IN THE VAPOR LIKE A FORTY-FOOT LIGHTED SWORD. "SPECIAL EFFECTS."

more difficult to trace, particularly since Andromeda is standing on her head. But a square is a square is a square, even to a small child, and when she follows your directions and looks up into the western sky, she's going to see a tipped-up-on-one-corner square—the Great Square—and you're off to a good start.

February

Snowflakes—No Two Alike?

We all know what happens when snow reaches us, but we may not know exactly what causes snow in the first place. What's the story here?

Basically, snow is water vapor that has condensed into ice crystals. As the water molecules cool, they stop bouncing off one another like Dodg'em cars, take up positions, and become relatively stable in groups of six, in hexagonal forms—ice crystals. The crystals usually form around infinitesimally small dust particles. As time passes, more and more water molecules condense into crystalline additions to the first crystal, and it grows. Everything going on around the crystal affects its development and the shape it will assume next: humidity, temperature, whether it is rising in the sky or falling through the clouds, and even the speed of descent. It all matters. Temperature probably has the greatest impact.

Some forms, like simple plates, are created in air near the freezing point. Others, like the spidery dendrites, occur at temperatures just above zero. There are ten recognized forms of snow crystals. A large flake may display several of these designs or may be the result of several flakes colliding on the way down to earth. Besides the plates and dendrites there are stellars, columns, needles, and capped columns. There have even been columnar flakes on which the columns were capped with crystals that looked like six-petaled flowers. There can be flakes of great beauty and complexity in almost any storm—you never know. The last time we had snow, I found some extremely long columnar flakes and four flakes designed exactly like a "single" rose—six round petals connected in the center to form a tiny flower.

There are questions—intriguing, important questions—about the development of snowflakes that still baffle physicists, but the question most kids ask is, "Are there ever two snowflakes alike?" The fact is, if you're talking about the molecular structure of a snowflake, the answer is probably no. No two snowflakes have ever been identical, because most snowflakes are complex and in a state of constant change. You could even say that no single flake is an identical match to the flake it was just five minutes ago. Speaking of snowflakes in *The Science of Everyday Life,* the author Jay Ingram says, ". . . the average water molecule in an ice crystal jumps out of its position once every millionth of a second, wanders a little way down the crystal, maybe a distance of eight molecules or so, then kicks another H_2O out of its place, and jumps back into the crystal."

If you mean, "I have about a hundred snowflakes on my coat right now, and some of them look alike to me" you may be right. It is possible that in a flurry of small, simple flakes there will be several that look the same to the naked eye.

Take the kids outdoors the next time it snows and see how many types of flakes you can find. Someone will have to wear a dark coat or bring a piece of black velvet or suede. Snow that fell on the ground or a tree ten minutes ago will have already changed noticeably; delicate details will have begun to merge with the snow mass. Wait ten minutes for your dark surface to become chilled before you attempt to "catch" flakes on it. Be careful not to breathe on your specimens, and use a magnifying glass. You can get one for under two dollars, but some of the small, inexpensive ones distort the subject greatly. You may want to try a "reading glass" instead. You can probably find one for seven or eight dollars. The glass is about two by four inches, in a tough plastic frame with a handle, and it is remarkably distortion-free. The difference in viewing is worth the difference in price.

ONLY ONE STATE IN THE CONTIGUOUS FORTY-EIGHT STATES AVERAGES AN INCH OR LESS OF SNOW EVERY YEAR—FLORIDA. FIVE STATES ARE SPLIT: HALF OF EACH OF THESE FIVE GETS AN INCH OR LESS, WHILE THE OTHER HALF RECEIVES UP TO 12 INCHES. THE REMAINING FORTY-TWO STATES GET 12 INCHES OR MORE IN THE AVERAGE YEAR, SOMETIMES A LOT MORE. BLUE CANYON, CALIFORNIA, GETS 240.8 INCHES; MARQUETTE, MICHIGAN, GETS 126.0. SAULT STE. MARIE, MICHIGAN, RECEIVES 116.4 INCHES. CARIBOU, MAINE, GETS 111.5, AND SYRACUSE, NEW YORK, GETS 110.5.

You'll use the reading glass for magnification over and over throughout the year.

Seed Catalogues and Pumpkin Magic

Seed catalogues are flooding the post offices now, and it's time to think about this year's garden. "Gardening"—it has a kind of serious, adult ring to it, doesn't it? But it doesn't have to be like that. There are all kinds of gardens, and there are lots of things you can do to make your kids' first gardening experiences memorable (in the nicest possible way).

Begin by thinking in terms of a child-size space. If a child's garden is too big for him or her to handle, it will turn into a jungle by midsummer. At that point it will irritate you every time you look at it, and it will embarrass the child to the point where he or she will use the front door exclusively rather than face it. Avoid this by figuring out how much garden you can handle all by yourself and then allot a small square of this to each child. When things such as summer camp, Little League, or the new puppy steal your assistants away, you will still be able to cope without feeling put upon, because right from the start you knew you could handle their gardens, and might have to. If they return to the project—and they very likely will if they can do so without feeling ashamed or overwhelmed—they can pick up where they left off. (This is not a perfect world, so if I were you, I would not expect thanks for keeping things going in their absence.)

If you're lucky, their little spot of garden will accomplish something more than producing fresh vegetables or flowers.

They will have the thrill of planting some little brown seeds and finding, ten days later, a whole row of tiny plants where the seeds went in. If they cared for the seedlings at all, even sporadically, they will experience real satisfaction as they pick their radishes or beans. Something buried deep in our collective species' memory rises to tingle just under the surface of consciousness when we harvest something we planted and tended to fruition, a special kind of pride or gratitude, or both. Maybe by the end of the season the kids will have acquired good feelings about growing things, and that's what really matters, because the world needs all the gardeners it can get.

It might also help if you have some fun with different vegetable varieties and experiment with planting arrangements. For instance, if you're going to have beans anyway, why not put up a bean pole teepee? Trim the branches off a dozen saplings or invest in a dozen bean or tomato poles (eight feet minimum). Gather everyone together to put up the teepee, because this is more than a one-man job. Set out these poles so they form a teepee shape, coming together at the top and separated on the north side of the circle to form an entrance. Jam each pole into the ground a couple of inches. Tie them all together at the top just about four or five inches from the pole ends. Does this structure look like a teepee to you? Then you have it right.

For a bean teepee, I recommend a pole bean variety with a pretty flower, preferably red. Some bean vines in flower are just beautiful. As soon as the vines start to bloom, you'll have a striking little structure out there in the garden. Once the vines are thoroughly leafed out, one or two children at a time can go into the teepee and sit of an afternoon, reading in the cool green shade. When the beans form, they will tend to hang down into the center of the teepee, which makes for easy picking and a very tender bean. You can even cut out a bright red or pink banner, letter the family name on it, and attach it to the top of the teepee when you first put it up.

If you would rather go for size, how about growing an eight-hundred-pound pumpkin? That eight hundred pounds is not a typographical error. Mr. Howard Dill of 400 College Road, Windsor, Nova Scotia B0N 2T0, Canada, has a patent on a giant pumpkin, and for a dollar he will send you a pumpkin catalogue with descriptions of pumpkins that can be held in the palm of your hand, the eight-hundred-pounders, and all sizes in between. Mr. Dill raises prizewinners regularly, and knows all there is to know about how to do it. Growing one of these giants is a family project. Sex is involved, and ruthless pruning, and the kind of care normally given premature babies. And—the kids will love this—there is always the possibility that your pumpkin might explode. Did you know there is a World Pumpkin Confederation? It sponsors contests and weigh-ins. You could be famous. You could have A Showing of the Pumpkin in your backyard on the first Sunday in October, from two to four. Friends and neighbors could come. The local paper might send a photographer. You could line everyone up beside the pumpkin, and take a snapshot, and send a copy to Charles Schulz of "Peanuts" fame. (Remember the Great Pumpkin?) People in your neighborhood will be talking about it for years to come. "No, Elsie, that was in late October. I distinctly remember it was after the Browns had their pumpkin showing."

Hand over those catalogues!

Snow Insulation and Real Central Heating

Were you aware that snow has great insulation capability? It certainly does. Theoretically speaking, there could be a 40- or 50-degree difference between the temperature of the air above a snow drift and the temperature deep inside the drift, if the outside air is cold enough. When the interior of a snow drift goes much over 32 degrees, you don't have snow any longer, you have water, so to get a 50-degree spread, you have to start with an air temperature of 15- to 20-degrees below zero, at least. Since you will probably be working with a low of no more than zero or 10 degrees below zero, your experiment won't produce such a fantastic spread, but it will be startling enough.

Bundle up the most restless youngsters in the family and hand them a good, sturdy outdoor thermometer. Be sure all the noses, fingers, and toes are protected against frostbite. (Try a thin coating of petroleum jelly on ears and noses.) Have them hang the thermometer on a shrub or low tree branch, out of the sun, for fifteen minutes to get an accurate air reading. Then have them push it two feet deep into the snow beneath the branch, or into a drift, and leave it there for at least fifteen minutes.

Most children will assume that the temperature deep within the snow will be even colder than the air above it. They may insist on repeating this experiment several times in different locations, in case someone is putting them on.

Later, over hot chocolate, you can explain. The center of the earth is incredibly hot, 9,000 degrees Fahrenheit. Some of our deeper mines—which, after all, do not go very deep, considering the distance between us and the center of the planet (3,960 miles, more or less)—are so hot that it is difficult for men to work in them for more than a few hours at a time. The temperature of the earth increases by 1 degree Centigrade for every one hundred feet you go down. Add to this central heating the warmth stored up in the earth's surface by the sun's rays. Now, over this toss a blanket of snow. Falling snow creates countless tiny air chambers as it lands and piles up, and all those billions of little trapped-air spaces serve as insulation. Perfectly still air does not conduct heat well, so a thick blanket of snow conserves whatever heat is in the soil beneath it.

It is kind of thought-provoking to stand there in the icy wind and look at a thermometer that has just been warmed in the middle of a snowbank by the core heat of the earth and stored heat from the sun. There's the proof—in tiny black numbers and a short red line.

From Sap to Syrup

The question for the dinner table forum tonight is "What do they harvest in late February and March in New England, parts of Canada, and states such as New York, Pennsylvania, and Michigan?" The answer is maple syrup. Well, actually, they harvest maple sap and then they slave over a hot evaporator to turn it into syrup.

If you don't usually have genuine maple syrup in the cupboard, buy a pint today, and maybe a small box of maple sugar candy. The kids should at least taste it to see what it's like. Children who don't eat many sweets may dislike the

candy at first; it is intensely sweet. Artificial maple flavor pales in comparison to the full-bodied real thing.

It takes a maple (usually the sugar maple, *Acer saccharum*) forty to fifty years to reach a size that will permit extensive tapping. A farmer who plants sugar maples today isn't doing it for himself. He's making an investment, he hopes, for his children and grandchildren.

Once the trees are in, he can't just walk off and leave the "sugar bush" to reach maturity on its own. The young trees must be watched for disease and insect infestation, and the land around them kept fairly clear. So that is forty or fifty years of caring and checking before he can reap a substantial harvest from his trees.

On the traditional sugar bush farms, fresh holes are bored into each producing tree, and spiles—hollow tubes through which the sap flows—are driven into the tree. Buckets are suspended from the spiles. The number of taps on a tree and their placement depends on a lot of factors, primarily the age of the tree. The number can range from one to six or seven (which is rare). On a less traditional sugar bush the sap travels through long tubes into central collection drums and is delivered to the sugarhouse through hosing or by truck.

Once the trees have been tapped, everything hinges on the weather. The sap runs best when the nights are cold (in the mid-twenties) and the days are bright and warm. No one can predict accurately what the yield will be. If the weather doesn't cooperate, the yield may be miserably small. If it does cooperate, a producer may have sap coming in faster than he can handle it. Once the maple buds start to swell, the syrup season is over.

The amount of sugar in the sap varies widely. It can take as many as fifty gallons of sap to produce one gallon of syrup. That is fifty—no mistake. Or in a good year it may take as few (?) as thirty. If the evaporator is wood-fired, it also takes cords and cords of wood to boil off all that water and make syrup.

The sap is usually boiled down in a sugarhouse. Before you go to maple country, contact the appropriate state department of agriculture or tourist board and ask for information about maple syrup producers. If possible, call the place you're going to visit before starting out in case the weather has shut the trees down temporarily. Given a choice, visit farms that still use spiles and buckets, and still boil off in wood-fired evaporators. Besides offering you a peek at the process, many of these places sell their own maple products, provide syrup-on-snow snacks (with pickles and doughnuts), and arrange for horse-drawn rides through the sugar bush.

When you open the sugarhouse door, if it's on a traditionally run farm, you will walk into something like a sweet Dante's Inferno. A massive wood fire is continually being fed under the evaporator, a tremendous rectangular metal pan that takes up most of the room. Sap vapor fills the place with mist. Sometimes the mist is so thick that the men working around the evaporator loom up suddenly in front of you and then disappear back into the cloud again an instant later. Shouted questions and instructions go back and forth over the steady muted roar of the fire and the pop-snap-splash of the bubbling sap. It's hot in there—hot and noisy and mysterious.

When the syrup reaches the proper density, it must be strained and graded and put into the waiting containers. Sometimes when the sap is flowing fast, work will go on most of the night and start again in the morning. You can't hold the sap back. Tomorrow it might stop flowing.

If you would like to try making some syrup yourself and have a big sugar maple or two in the yard, give it a shot. You will find spiles or spouts at rural hardware and feed stores in maple syrup country in January and February. You'll also need as many one-gallon plastic milk jugs, with their caps, as you can save up. And you'll need a way to cook off most of the water in the sap outdoors and something to cook it in, such as a big roasting pan. Perhaps you could rig a temporary stove out of cement blocks and a stone-lined fire pit or use a camp cookstove. And you'll need a candy thermometer. That's very important.

Your trees should be big enough to take tapping—at least ten inches in diameter. A tree ten inches to eighteen inches in diameter can support one tap. From eighteen inches to twenty-four inches, try two taps. A really massive tree can take three or four, but better less than more since you are not an experienced tapper. But do not tap a tree that is ailing.

Put one spile in early in the season as a sort of test case. Drill a hole for the spile about an inch and a half into the wood, making the hole two or three inches deep in all, counting the bark. Drill at a slight angle upward so the sap will just naturally flow down into your jug. When the spile is in place, give it a little smack with your hammer to set it firmly. As soon as you see sap running from that first spout, put the rest of them out.

You can buy regular sap buckets for this operation, but gallon milk jugs seem to work quite well on a small scale. Cut a

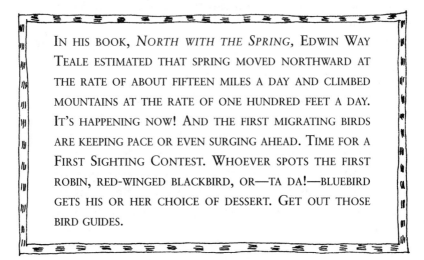

IN HIS BOOK, *NORTH WITH THE SPRING*, EDWIN WAY TEALE ESTIMATED THAT SPRING MOVED NORTHWARD AT THE RATE OF ABOUT FIFTEEN MILES A DAY AND CLIMBED MOUNTAINS AT THE RATE OF ONE HUNDRED FEET A DAY. IT'S HAPPENING NOW! AND THE FIRST MIGRATING BIRDS ARE KEEPING PACE OR EVEN SURGING AHEAD. TIME FOR A FIRST SIGHTING CONTEST. WHOEVER SPOTS THE FIRST ROBIN, RED-WINGED BLACKBIRD, OR—TA DA!—BLUEBIRD GETS HIS OR HER CHOICE OF DESSERT. GET OUT THOSE BIRD GUIDES.

hole in a clean milk jug an inch or so below the top of the neck and hang the jug on the spile through that hole. Since your jug is capped, very little foreign matter will get into your sap.

Set your taps in the southern side of your tree if possible and place them in line with big roots or big branches. Collect the sap late in the day if you can so it won't freeze in the jug overnight. If it does, you'll have to hang another jug in its place while the first one thaws out.

If you are going to cook the sap down on the weekend, you'll have to store what you collect during the week in a covered container, in a very cool spot.

Improvise a cooking setup. The idea is to fill a roasting pan or similar container with at least two inches of sap; to cook the sap until it gives up most of its water content; and then to bottle it in sterilized, capped jars. The temperature of the cooking sap will let you know when it's ready to be bottled. Commercial operators produce different grades of syrup and use more complicated indicators, but the amateur goes by temperature.

While the sap is boiling away, watch it carefully so it will not scorch. It is customary to rig a big bucket of sap over the evaporator so a thin trickle of fresh sap constantly flows into the evaporator, but for your first experiment with syrup, this may be more than you want to tackle. Instead, just set aside a long morning or afternoon, stay by your evaporator, and whenever the level of sap starts to drop in the pan, add more fresh sap until you run out of sap, your arms give out, or your feet go numb. At that point you can finish the process indoors, because you've already gotten most of the water out of your sap.

Pour what's left in your evaporator into a *big* pot (eight quarts, perhaps) and put it on the stove. Using a candy thermometer (which you have checked recently for accuracy by placing it in a pot of boiling water), take the temperature of the syrup every few minutes. When it goes above boiling—212 degrees—hover over that pot like a mother hen. When the temperature reaches 219 or 220, it's done! As it approaches that point it will probably boil up—just suddenly rise in the pan as if it were going to explode. Touch the top of the boil with a tiny bit of butter or bacon on the end of a knife to make it subside. Take it off the stove and pour it into your hot sterilized jars. Most people like to filter their syrup as they pour it.

Why do all that boiling outdoors when you have a perfectly good stove sitting in the kitchen, which is warm and dry, and it's freezing outside? If you do all your boiling down in the kitchen, gallons of water vapor will be released indoors, and your wallpaper will come down in strips, your paint will peel, and the kitchen woodwork will feel like the inside of an empty jam jar. If you do most of your boiling outdoors, the remaining water vapor will dissipate harmlessly inside.

The Biggest Dog You'll Ever See —Canis Major

Some clear night in February, after everyone has had a hearty, warming kind of dinner, take them all outdoors to meet a very Big Dog.

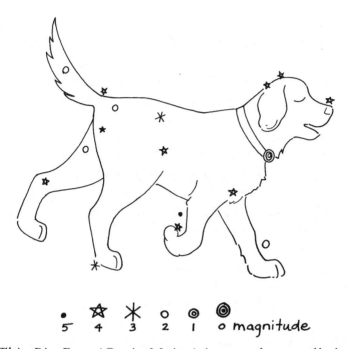

This Big Dog (Canis Major) is not always all there. Sometimes if the night is not very clear, his fainter stars are hard to see. But to make up for that, the Big Dog wears the Dog Star—Sirius—on his collar. Sirius is the brightest star in our sky. It is one of the closest also, being only eight and a half light-years away. (A light-year is the distance that light would travel in one solar year—approximately 5,878,000,000,000 miles; or to put it another way, five trillion eight hundred and seventy-eight billion miles.)

Early on a February evening you will find the Big Dog in the southern part of the sky, not too far above the horizon. There are several bright stars to outline his hindquarters and tail, and another to mark his forepaw. He looks as if he is trotting up into the sky alongside the Milky Way. His paws are on his southwestern side, his back, head, and tail on his eastern side. You should have no trouble finding Sirius. But at some point there may be mutinous mutterings from the smaller members. The muttering may become a rumble and a voice may pipe up: "Well, that's not the brightest star up there, I don't care what Daddy says. I see a brighter one right over there." The kid points, and lo, he's right. There really is something brighter over there.

Since Sirius truly is the brightest star, unless a cloud is obscuring it, the kid has just spotted a planet. Time to turn to June and read up on planets.

March

Where Does the Wind Come From?

March being the windy month, you may be asked to explain wind. You could say that wind is the movement of air around the earth, which is quite correct. But someone is sure to ask, "What makes the air move?" Ah, thereby hangs a tale.

We begin with the sun heating the earth, its land masses and its bodies of water. There are infinite variations in how the earth's surfaces handle this solar energy. Ocean water reflects back about 40 percent of the heat it receives; soil absorbs the heat and releases it back into the air by radiation; the air over warm water becomes warmer through contact, and so on. The bottom line is that because of those variations, the air becomes unevenly heated. That's the big engine that creates wind—the uneven heating of air.

Gases—and air is a mixture of gases—will always react to or reconcile temperature differences by moving. As the air over heated ground gets hotter, its molecules become more and more active; they speed up and spread out. Heated air expands, gets lighter, and rises. The denser, cooler air around it, which is heavier, rushes in to fill the space being vacated. The rising of heated air is called convection. The cooler air flowing toward the warmer spot is wind.

The air around the equator is, of course, constantly being heated and constantly rising. The air over the Arctic is con-

The Beaufort Wind Scale*
(m.p.h. of wind)

stantly cooling and falling. You can probably guess what the result is. A flow is set up whereby the cool air over the Arctic region creeps southward toward the equator where the air is constantly rising, turning north, and heading for the Arctic. This is referred to as the Hadley circulation, in honor of the gentleman who "discovered" it in 1735. There is more to it, of course. The earth is turning on its axis once every twenty-four hours, and all that motion puts its own spin on every weather system. The fact that the earth's axis is tilted, resulting in our seasons, complicates everything. And there is the never-ending commotion between low-pressure areas and high-pressure areas. Air will always escape from high-pres-

*For more information on the Beaufort Wind Scale, see page 147.

sure areas to low-pressure areas as fast as possible. Untie the mouth of an inflated balloon (high pressure) and watch it zoom around the room powered solely by the thrust of its own high-pressure air escaping into the low-pressure air of the room. Every time a tire goes flat we are dealing with the consequences of the same process.

Even the textures of the earth's surface (mountain ranges, deserts, large bodies of water) make a difference, and cities and heavily wooded areas can modify the weather over and around them. (The more you study weather, the more you understand the meteorologist's need to rely on computers to process all the data coming in to his office every day.)

If I were explaining all this to a very young child, in the end I'd say, "Hot air goes up, like the smoke in our chimney, and the cold air hurries in to take its place, and what we feel flowing past us today is probably cooler air on its way to another warmer spot."

The older kids might get a kick out of making a Bull-roarer or Thunderstick, an old-fashioned toy that creates its own wind and, in the process, some very weird wind sounds.

Find a short ruler or piece of wood about six or eight inches

THERE IS A PRINCIPLE—BUYS BALLOT'S LAW (APPLYING ONLY TO THE NORTHERN HEMISPHERE)—THAT SAYS IF YOU STAND WITH YOUR BACK TO THE WIND, THE AREA OF HIGH PRESSURE WILL BE ON YOUR RIGHT AND THE AREA OF LOW PRESSURE WILL BE ON YOUR LEFT. TRY IT AND SEE IF YOUR RESULTS AGREE WITH THE METEOROLOGIST'S WEATHER MAP ON TELEVISION.

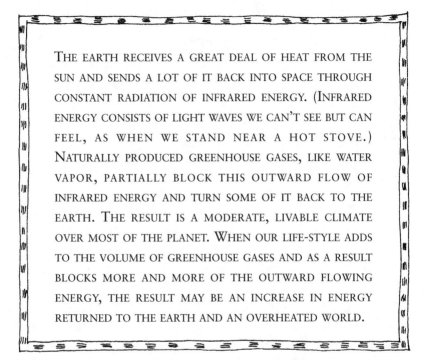

THE EARTH RECEIVES A GREAT DEAL OF HEAT FROM THE SUN AND SENDS A LOT OF IT BACK INTO SPACE THROUGH CONSTANT RADIATION OF INFRARED ENERGY. (INFRARED ENERGY CONSISTS OF LIGHT WAVES WE CAN'T SEE BUT CAN FEEL, AS WHEN WE STAND NEAR A HOT STOVE.) NATURALLY PRODUCED GREENHOUSE GASES, LIKE WATER VAPOR, PARTIALLY BLOCK THIS OUTWARD FLOW OF INFRARED ENERGY AND TURN SOME OF IT BACK TO THE EARTH. THE RESULT IS A MODERATE, LIVABLE CLIMATE OVER MOST OF THE PLANET. WHEN OUR LIFE-STYLE ADDS TO THE VOLUME OF GREENHOUSE GASES AND AS A RESULT BLOCKS MORE AND MORE OF THE OUTWARD FLOWING ENERGY, THE RESULT MAY BE AN INCREASE IN ENERGY RETURNED TO THE EARTH AND AN OVERHEATED WORLD.

long, maybe two inches wide, and not more than half an inch thick. Drill a hole in one end and attach the wood to a stout cord or thong about four feet long. Make sure that no one is standing behind you—*that is very important*—and then start spinning the piece of wood around your head as if it were a cowboy's lariat. With a little practice you can get some impressive wind sounds out of your Bull-roarer. It is the same basic principle as the wind moaning around the eaves of the house—air moving fast past an obstacle—except that this time the obstacle is moving fast through the air, creating its own wind.

How Does the Wind Lift Our Kites?

*T*he trick to getting a kite up, and keeping it up, is flying it at an angle. You tilt the kite at an angle to "catch" the wind, which will push it upward and downwind simultaneously when the angle is right. The force of the wind is counteracted by the downward-upwind pull you exert through the kite string and bridle, and the weight of the kite's tail. A constantly shifting equilibrium is set up and maintained as long as the wind continues to blow.

You can't fly a kite perpendicular or parallel to the earth because it would not "catch" the wind that way—the wind would either shear straight up or flow right over it, exerting no push.

When the wind dies down, you instinctively start to run backward, trying to create a temporary "wind" that way, and save the situation. Eventually, of course, either the wind picks up again or you drop to the ground about ten seconds before your kite does, and that's all for both of you.

Try making this slightly different kite. (You will need a special location to fly it—a place where the wind is likely to blow steadily all through the night, such as a shoreline, hilltop, or lake front—so settle on your site first. The normal kite safety rules will apply—such as, don't fly this kite near an airport, power lines, or, particularly in this case, a busy street.) Construct a very large, sturdy kite out of dark materials—black plastic, perhaps, the kind they sell for mulching or construction use or the kind you find in huge trash bags. Attach three or four Light Sticks* to the kite string near the kite or at the outer corners of the kite frame, whichever works best for you. Experiment by actually flying the kite with the sticks attached before you "light" them.

When the kite is ready to go, and it is dark outdoors, bend the sticks to start them glowing and send that kite up. Anchor the string securely to a piling or a fence post, and walk away clean. The kite won't show at night but the Light Sticks will, floating way up there in the darkness, glowing eerily. The effect is marvelous. Passersby are sure to do a double or triple take. The first impression is that there is a U.F.O. up there. Frequently a small crowd will gather. And the local sporting goods store is sure to do a brisk business in Light Sticks the following day.

With any luck your kite will still be up there when the sun rises, riding the winds of morning like a black hawk.

*Slender, flexible plastic rods filled with chemicals that interact to produce a cool green or blue light when you bend the rods.

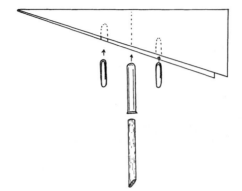

Wind Vanes, Large and Small
—Very Small

Maybe some Saturday afternoon the kids would like to construct their own wind vane. It's easy and inexpensive, and this model works just as well as the $200 ones. Better. Spare parts are so easy to get.

You will need one empty milk carton, two paper clips, one ¼-inch dowel two to four feet long, and the top or bottom of a thermometer case or half an empty ballpoint pen.

Thermometers are always coming to a splintery end on the bathroom floor or in the sink. The cases are practically indestructible. There should be a spare case hiding out in a drawer in the kitchen.

Cut two identical, long, thin wedges or triangles out of the sides of the milk carton. Lay them down with their long sides matched and closest to you.

Place the empty thermometer case between the triangles—a little closer to the narrow, tip end of the wedge than to the wide end. Fasten a paper clip on each side of the thermometer case so that it is firmly held between the triangles, with its open end extending down below the matched edges of the triangles. There is your wind vane.

Select a site for the vane where buildings, trees, and fences will have the least possible influence on it. Stick your dowel into the ground and slip the open end of the thermometer case down over the top of the dowel. Your new wind vane should spin around and settle down pointed into the breeze.

If the wind gets high enough, your vane may take off and come to rest twenty feet downwind. No problem. Just slip it back on the dowel.

The earliest wind vanes in this country were not the lovely big copper, brass, or iron running horses or sailing ships that are so valued today. They were quite basic—a piece of old cloth tied to a stick, for example. (How's that for "basic"?) The collectors' vanes that command such astounding prices today were a feature of later, more elaborate homes. I guess ours would fall somewhere in between.

If you would like to work in miniature or determine which way the softest summer breeze is blowing, collect a spider web, fasten it to a dry grass stalk or a small, upright stick, and then fasten a parachute-type seed such as a dandelion seed to the end of the web that is still floating free. *Voilà!* A wind vane for the chipmunks in the garden.

Peeptoads—Singing in the Swamp

$\mathcal{S}$ometime in the next few weeks if you live in the Peeptoad Triangle (from New Brunswick, Canada, south to South Carolina and then northwest through Michigan to Manitoba), you will probably hear the first peeptoads, or spring peepers, of the season. No one can say exactly when they will start singing. Average temperature seems to be the single most important factor. Some naturalists believe it has to be about 50 degrees before frogs and toads respond, but our experience has been that lots of frogs and toads can't wait that long. They take up their positions in the swamp and start singing when the average temperature is still well below 50 degrees.

The peeptoad is actually a frog and is scientifically known as *Hyla crucifer.* H.C. is a little fellow, about an inch long. He has a powerful voice for one so small. He comes in shades of gray, soft brown, and olive green. The *crucifer* in his Latin name refers to a cross marking on his back. When H.C. sings, he keeps his mouth closed (which makes the volume of his song all the more amazing), but an area of white skin under his chin inflates to form a big white bubble.

He spend his winters in the woods under a protective cover of leaves, litter, and earth. When the ice on ponds and swamps melts, he knows it. He climbs out and heads for the water. Upon reaching the pond, he launches himself into courtship and starts a new generation of peeptoads. His singing is a part of the courtship ritual, and when the reproductive cycle has run its course, H.C. quiets right down. He will leave the pond then and spend the rest of the summer in woodsy places. Although he is a tree frog, he usually hunts for the very small insects he eats on the ground or in low, shrubby thickets. Once in a while, however, he will be discovered way up in a tree. Nature equipped him with small discs on his feet, and he can climb like a son of a gun.

If the kids would like to see H.C. performing during the courtship season, arm everyone with boots (for the boggy spots), insect repellent, and flashlights. When you first approach the pond, you can expect every little peeper to stop singing. This becomes a waiting game. Just pick your spot near the edge of the water and relax. Ardor will eventually win out over common sense, and the peepers will start to sing again. Look for those white bubbles. They show up at night. Concentrate on spots where brush or grasses arch out over the water, providing protective cover.

After the peepers have been singing for some days or weeks, they will sing just as lustily during the day as they do at night, and if you don't mind getting a little muddy, you can probably flush some out of the leaves and litter floating at the edge of a pond or off a little hillock at the edge of the marsh.

When someone comes in of an evening and announces that he or she has heard the peepers, everyone knows spring has come to the swamp.

The Vernal Equinox —Countdown to Spring

March 21, give or take a few hours, is the spring, or vernal, equinox. *Equinox* is one of those words that everyone recognizes but not everyone fully understands. The kids may hear it mentioned but not explained on the evening weather report. So in line with our policy of having all the answers ready as long as someone asks the right questions, here we go.

Equinox comes from the Latin words for equal and night. At the time of the equinox (there are two every year—on or about March 21 and on or about September 22), day and night are supposed to be exactly equal in length—twelve hours each. It is the moment when the sun crosses the celestial equator, in the case of the vernal equinox, heading north. On December 22, give or take a few hours, it reached its farthest point south of the equator and has been returning northward ever since. The farther north it comes, the shorter our nights and the longer our days. March 21 marks the halfway point on its northern swing.

June 21 (this varies by a few hours from year to year) is the summer solstice, the date on which it reaches its greatest distance north of the celelestial equator. It is hard to believe, but from then on, all through the summer, the days are actually getting shorter.

If you consult an almanac, you may notice that at 40 degrees latitude the day of March 21 is described as twelve hours and eight or nine minutes long. "How come?" you may well ask. Two reasons: We count daylight as beginning with the first glimpse of the rising sun and ending with the last glimpse of the setting sun. Since it takes several minutes for the sun to rise and to set, you pick up a little extra daylight there. Also, due to the action of the earth's atmosphere, the sun's rays are bent; they come to us at an angle. This means that we see the sun's rays before they actually come up over the horizon. A minute here, a minute there—it adds up.

If the kids don't ask about the equinox, bring it up. No point in hiding your light under a bushel.

The equinox doesn't call for an experiment as much as it calls for a celebration. Have an Equinox Experience. Serve sandwiches made with one slice of pumpernickel and one slice of white bread. Wash them down with root beer and vanilla ice cream floats. For dessert, put together a cake that is half chocolate and half vanilla or has one layer of each. (I know this meal is heavy on carbohydrates and sugar. You don't stage a celebration with carrot sticks and broccoli.) For a centerpiece, how about one six-inch white candle (six months of long days) and one six-inch dark candle (six months of long nights)? The actual moment of the equinox passing is usually some odd little time like 4:33 in the afternoon or the morning when no one is up or no one is home. I say let's observe it as the sun goes down on the day of the equinox. You can check the time of sunset in the newspaper. "Ladies and gentlemen, we are now counting down: ten . . . nine . . . eight . . . seven . . . six . . . five . . . four . . . three . . . two . . . one . . . *Spring*!"

Gemini, the Stardust Twins

*T*ake the kids out to meet the Twins some soft March night. Castor and Pollux, otherwise known as Gemini, will be dancing down the Milky Way right over your heads. Since they will be very high in the sky, you might stretch out on quilts or on the hood of the car, or lie on summer lounge chairs. It is dizzying to stand and stare straight up for any length of time, and it hurts the neck.

All the directions in this book for locating stars are given for an observer living near the 40th latitude (see page 20 for a discussion of latitudes) during the hour after dusk. If you're stargazing near the 30th latitude, in line with Jacksonville, Florida, or Houston, Texas, the Twins will be a little farther south than I describe them.

Face south. Look straight up and then just a shade to the southwest of the zenith (which is the spot directly over you,

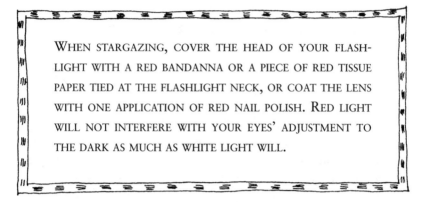

WHEN STARGAZING, COVER THE HEAD OF YOUR FLASH-
LIGHT WITH A RED BANDANNA OR A PIECE OF RED TISSUE
PAPER TIED AT THE FLASHLIGHT NECK, OR COAT THE LENS
WITH ONE APPLICATION OF RED NAIL POLISH. RED LIGHT
WILL NOT INTERFERE WITH YOUR EYES' ADJUSTMENT TO
THE DARK AS MUCH AS WHITE LIGHT WILL.

wherever you are). You should see two bright stars, Castor and Pollux. Pollux will be a yellow star. These stars represent the Twins' heads.

Now look for an uneven line of five smaller stars south and southwest of Castor and Pollux, which suggests arms, as if the Twins were holding hands. These stars are not very bright, but there's not too much else up there to confuse you.

When we get down to the hips, legs, and feet, you may have to study the picture above you for a few minutes. The ecliptic—the planets' pathway—slices right through the hip area, and the Twins' feet are twinkling down the Milky Way. Oddly enough, this puts a city dweller at a distinct advantage. He may not be able to see much of the Milky Way because of air pollution, but the six stars that represent the feet of the Twins will stand out. Someone looking through a very clear atmosphere will see thousands and thousands of stars in the Milky Way and may find it harder to pick out the Twins' feet.

When you feel that you really know the Twins well, the kids might enjoy meeting the Little Dog. It seems appropriate that he tags along behind the Twins like a friendly puppy. Look to the south of the Twins. You should see one small, bright star and one quite large star. They will line up on an axis pointing south-southeast to west-northwest. The bigger, brighter star will be south of its smaller brother. These two stars are the Little Dog (Canis Minor). There's no way you can make a whole dog out of two stars, but that's what the constellation is called, so we must use our imagination to fill in the rest of the dog.

The bigger of these two stars in Canis Minor is Procyon, a zero magnitude star. Pollux is a first magnitude star, and Castor is a second magnitude star. First magnitude and zero magnitude stars are the biggest and brightest we see. There are only twenty-one of them, and they stand out so clearly that you will get to know them before the year is out. Stars are ranked by brightness, from 0 and 1 to 5, and so on. Fifth magnitude stars are visible to the naked eye only under good conditions; they are very faint. Sixth magnitude stars are usually so dim that you need glasses or a telescope to see them.

Once the kids get to know most of the easy, interesting constellations, the night skies really will be "friendly skies" for them. Learning to spot their favorites will take time—several sessions a month, maybe, through the year—but each session can be quite short. If everyone has a good time, drinking cocoa or lemonade, taking turns with the star book and the flashlight, and if you can diplomatically give a little help when it's needed so that no one feels foolish for not being able to see right away what everyone else sees, the kids will acquire a feeling for the stars and the night that should last a lifetime.

April

"Water, Water, Everywhere . . ."

When the Ancient Mariner said that, he was drifting across the sea, dying of thirst. It doesn't take long. We can go maybe two months without food, but we cannot survive more than a week, if that, without water. If something were seriously to affect the purity or availability of our water resources, all our lives would be threatened. Furthermore, what gets into the water in Cleveland, Ohio, will eventually make a difference in Charleston, South Carolina, because water is constantly on the move and is very hard to break down. Once two hydrogen atoms combine with one oxygen atom, they will stay bonded together unless the water molecule they have formed is heated to 2900 degrees Celsius, which doesn't happen very often in the normal course of events. It is possible, therefore, and even probable, that water created three billion years ago is still coming out of our taps, still flowing in our rivers, still splashing on our feet at the seashore.

We are more water than anything else. It is a wonder we don't slosh with every step. More than 90 percent of our blood is liquid. It is less salty than the ocean, where all life began, but to this day the proportions of sodium to potassium and calcium in our blood are almost exactly what they are in salt water. A person suffering from dehydration is given water intravenously, and salt is added to the solution to preserve the proper balance. Even our bones are 22 percent water, and our brains are 75 percent fluid. We are all little inland seas.

And this is true of all the organisms around us. The things we eat, for instance, are surprisingly liquid. Our "solids" aren't solid at all; they contain a fairly high percentage of water. That raw steak you paid $6.99 a pound for was over 60 percent water. That substantial-looking potato on your plate is probably three-fourths liquid. Water is here, water is there—it's everywhere!

In fact, H_2O is the only common, abundant substance that is present naturally in all three states: liquid, solid (ice), and gaseous (water vapor). It is one of the very few substances to defy the general rule that as matter gets colder, it shrinks. Water does contract until its temperature is almost down to the freezing point, and then it begins to expand. It expands still further as it freezes and becomes capable of floating as ice. This departure from S.O.P. is a lifesaver for us. Suppose that as it cooled water did not expand and float. Every pond, river, and ocean in the colder climates would fill with successive layers of ice from the bottom up. This ice would not melt readily because it would be protected from the influence of the sun and warmer air by the chilled water directly over it. Eventually, there would be a great deal more ice than water in some areas of the planet, and a lot of moisture would be taken out of weather circulation. Much of the moderating effect of the water vapor in the air would be lost, and the outlook for the future of human life on this planet would not be good. So we live at the bottom of a protective, life-sustaining ocean of moist air. We eat, drink, and are, to a great extent, water.

Do the kids understand why things float in water? Water has considerable weight. One cubic centimeter weighs one gram. If what you are trying to float weighs more than the water it displaces, it will sink. If it weighs less, it will stay up, buoyed by its own lightness. Other factors may enter into it, such as surface tension, but displacement is the bottom line. So when you're loading a cargo ship, how do you know when to stop? If the man who designed the ship drew a line inside it and said, "Don't pile the cargo above this line," and he was thinking of a cargo of Styrofoam boxes but you were actually piling up steel ingots, the boat would have sunk like a rock long before you reached his line. Suppose, however, the designer drew a line on the outside of the boat and said, "Stop adding cargo when the water reaches this line," you'd know when enough was enough whether you were loading steel or Styrofoam. Fortunately, boat designers do draw such lines; they are called Plimsoll marks (or load lines) after the man who convinced everyone to use them, Samuel Plimsoll. Maybe the kids would like to draw some Plimsoll lines of their own on their own small ships. Their ships can be made of modeling clay or foil-covered cardboard or plastic. Their harbor can be the bathtub or the sink. They can load their ships with marbles, grapes, or whatever; at some point one more will be one more too many. Experience will show them where that point is, and they can draw a Plimsoll mark on their own boat with waterproof ink or a sharp point (adult supervision required).

In oceans and rivers, water temperature and salinity can vary and affect how much cargo a ship can safely load, so a Plimsoll mark takes all these factors into account, and it looks like this.

Key

AB STANDS FOR THE OFFICIAL LOAD LINE SET BY THE AMERICAN
BUREAU OF SHIPPING. ON THE SYMBOL ON THE RIGHT,

TF = TROPICAL FRESH WATER

F = FRESH WATER

T = TROPICAL SEAS

S = SUMMER SEAS

W = WINTER SEAS

WNA = WINTER, NORTH ATLANTIC

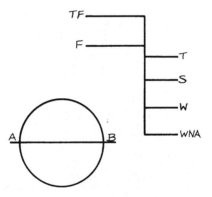

Ask the kids why it should matter whether the ship is sailing in fresh or salt water and what temperature the water is. What difference could that make if you were loading a ship? Clues: Salt water weighs more than fresh, per cubic foot; cold water is denser and therefore weighs more than warm water. As a result, cold salt water weighs most of all and will support more weight. The water in the North Atlantic is very cold and the saltiest of all the commonly sailed oceans, so it is capable of supporting more weight per cubic foot than most

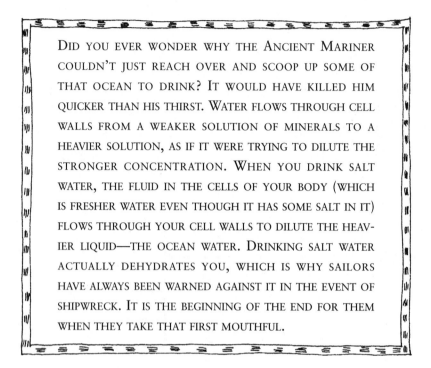

DID YOU EVER WONDER WHY THE ANCIENT MARINER COULDN'T JUST REACH OVER AND SCOOP UP SOME OF THAT OCEAN TO DRINK? IT WOULD HAVE KILLED HIM QUICKER THAN HIS THIRST. WATER FLOWS THROUGH CELL WALLS FROM A WEAKER SOLUTION OF MINERALS TO A HEAVIER SOLUTION, AS IF IT WERE TRYING TO DILUTE THE STRONGER CONCENTRATION. WHEN YOU DRINK SALT WATER, THE FLUID IN THE CELLS OF YOUR BODY (WHICH IS FRESHER WATER EVEN THOUGH IT HAS SOME SALT IN IT) FLOWS THROUGH YOUR CELL WALLS TO DILUTE THE HEAVIER LIQUID—THE OCEAN WATER. DRINKING SALT WATER ACTUALLY DEHYDRATES YOU, WHICH IS WHY SAILORS HAVE ALWAYS BEEN WARNED AGAINST IT IN THE EVENT OF SHIPWRECK. IT IS THE BEGINNING OF THE END FOR THEM WHEN THEY TAKE THAT FIRST MOUTHFUL.

other areas of the sea and large rivers, and that is why it is given its own special designation. A load of ten tons in WNA water will permit a ship to ride higher in the water than it would in TF water. Could that cause problems?

It Rained and It Rained. How Much Did It Rain?

April is not always the rainiest month. Actually, except for those states between the Mississippi River and the Appalachian Mountains, from the Gulf of Mexico to the Great Lakes, April is hardly ever the wettest month. But there is that familiar "April Showers" image, so let's talk about rain.

Rain is one of the links in something called the hydrologic cycle, which means the constant circulation of water around, over, and under the earth. Rain falls from a cloud into a river or ocean, or it falls on land and runs off into a stream, or it soaks into the earth and becomes part of the water table. Eventually, it all flows to the sea (even the water underground reaches the surface again at some point), and sooner or later it will be sucked up from the sea into the air by evaporation, become water vapor, and, under the right conditions, part of a cloud, which is where we came in. Sometimes the cycle takes a long, long time—water trapped in a glacier for centuries, for instance. Sometimes it is completed in only a few hours: A morning shower fills a ditch; under the influence of the summer sun, the ditch dries up and the water evaporates, and that vapor rises into a sky filling with late-afternoon thunderheads; the clouds grow, the storm breaks, and rain falls, filling the ditch.

Of course no natural process is that simple, not even the hydrologic cycle. Take those clouds, for instance. Water vapor rises through the air until it hits the higher levels where the air is cool. As it cools, air loses some of its ability to hold water vapor. (Warm air holds more moisture than cold air.) Sooner or later, air temperature dips to the point at which some vapor will condense into water droplets. Think of those water droplets as cloud droplets. When you go above the condensation level, you're in cloud country.

Each water droplet has formed around something. It needed something to condense onto. At ground level we see water vapor condensed on blades of grass and spider webs as morning dew. Up where the clouds are, it condenses around tiny particles—specks of dust and pollen, infinitesimal bits and pieces of atmospheric litter. It is estimated that there are one thousand to one million of them in each cubic inch of air overhead, depending on conditions at the moment, so there is always something at hand for water vapor to condense onto.

The resulting cloud droplets are so small that they would never fall to the ground, or anywhere else for that matter. They would just drift along as part of the cloud or wander off until they hit drier air and evaporated. They are less than $\frac{1}{1,000}$ of an inch in diameter. But a cloud droplet can serve as the "something" that surrounding water vapor needs to condense onto, and it can grow as a result of condensation going on around it. When it gets big enough, heavy enough, it will start to descend, and as it does, it will collide with other drops. The drops will adhere to one another in a process called coalescence until a raindrop has been created. Approximately one million cloud droplets make one raindrop (which is $\frac{1}{16}$ of an inch or more in diameter).

If the air between the clouds and the earth is quite dry and cool, the cloud droplets may never have the opportunity to coalesce as they would in a warmer, moister climate, and you may not end up with rain at all; you may get drizzle instead.

Having grappled with the creation of the individual raindrop, let us now move on to measuring raindrops in quantity and construct a rain gauge. It is not difficult or expensive to make. As soon as it is installed, the heavens will probably open and pour all month long, breaking all records and refuting everything we ever said about April not being the rainiest month, because Nature is not on the side of parents. If she were, would two-year-olds have an eight-foot reach? I think not. But if gully-washers should follow, they will at least give

the kids plenty to measure on their new rain gauge.

You will need the following: bright nail polish or waterproof paint, a ruler, a widemouthed, straight-sided jar (perhaps a Mason jar), a narrow, straight-sided bottle (perhaps an olive jar), two pieces of light wire about eighteen inches long each, one eighteen-inch piece of aluminum foil, one toothpick, and a straight branch or dowel about eighteen inches long.

Pour water into the widemouthed jar until it is one inch deep, then pour that water into the tall, narrow bottle. Mark the new water level using nail polish on a toothpick. You have converted one inch of liquid in a wide container into several inches in a narrow one. Rainfall measurement in fractions of an inch will be magnified and much easier to see in the narrow bottle.

To make it even easier to gauge the rainfall, divide the space between your nail polish mark and the bottom of the narrow bottle in half, and label that point ½ inch. Divide the spaces between the half-inch mark and the bottom of the bottle, and the half-inch mark and the one-inch mark in half, and label them ¼ inch and ¾ inch respectively.

Drive your dowel or branch several inches into the ground in a spot where nothing above it will interfere with rainfall. Wrap one end of a piece of wire around the top of the narrow bottle, place the bottle upright about four or five inches away from the dowel, and wrap the other end of the wire around the dowel. Now you have your marked bottle resting on the ground several inches to one side of its support.

Fold your foil in half lengthwise. Wrap one folded edge around the top of the widemouthed jar and join the free edges where they meet, folding them over and over to form a seal. This should give you a foil sleeve as wide across and as round as the jar. Take your second piece of wire and run it around the free end of this sleeve, rolling the foil over the wire as you go so that you end up with a foil sleeve suspended from a wire loop and attached at the other end to a jar. Slip the sleeve off the jar. Twist the wire ends together to hold them in place and attach the leftover ends to the dowel so that the foil sleeve will hang directly over the narrow bottle. Gently compress the lower end of the sleeve until it fits into and fills the mouth of the narrow bottle. Now you have a foil funnel collecting rain in its open mouth and delivering it into a narrow bottle that has been calibrated to measure water in quarter inches.

Let it rain—you're ready!

Tree Flowers . . . Pine Flowers?

Next time you're waiting
and waiting and waiting for your dinner at a restaurant, and
the waitress is working at a pace that suggests she expects to
get tipped by the hour and not by the order, ask the kids what
oak flowers look like. Or pine flowers. They will probably
give you the fish eye, because who ever heard of oak or pine
flowers? These are trick questions, right?

Not so. Many big trees actually bear two kinds of flowers,
as does the oak. One is quite inconspicuous, but the other is
not. In fact, once you become aware of it, you'll wonder how
you could have missed seeing it all these years. The oak bears
long, slender catkins that sway with the lightest breeze—oak
tassels, we might call them. They are the "male" flowers and
disperse the oak pollen. A big, healthy oak will literally be
hung with them, and the ground under such a tree will be
covered with discarded catkins for weeks in the spring. The
female oak flowers are small, inconspicuous clusters, and they
are the ones that eventually produce acorns.

Many maple trees flaunt beautiful little clusters of flowers in
April. Those on the silver and red maples are a rich red. From
a distance the trees look as if they are giving off a wine-col-
ored haze. Sugar maple flowers are a vibrant chartreuse.
When you stand under a flowering maple, see if you can pick
up a fragrance. Sugar maples smell like lemon-and-lime
candy. Kids have such sharp senses, they should be able to
catch that sweet smell.

Many willows produce catkins. A catkin is a spike of uni-
sexual flowers—very tiny flowers, usually—without petals.
Willows bloom before the leaves come out or just as they
unfold; the exact time varies from species to species.

The kids may go along with oak trees blooming, and willows and even maples, but some of them are going to balk at the idea of pine trees blooming. Well, those pinecones aren't just nailed up there by the Pine Fairy, you know. Pinecones are really very unusual seed holders. They are stuffed with small, winged seeds, and those seeds started with flowers. I'll admit that the word *flower* as applied to the pine is apt to promise more than it can deliver. The pine blooms in a very utilitarian fashion. There are male and female flowers, both shaped like small cones, on the same tree. The male flowers release clouds of pollen in season. We have seen pine pollen blowing across the road like yellow smoke in the late spring. We honestly wondered if the woods were on fire. If you come out to your car one morning and find it looking as if someone had dusted it with sulfur or curry powder, you're probably looking at pine pollen.

Many tree flowers are pretty enough to be included in bouquets, particularly the maples. And all of them are interesting when viewed through a magnifying glass. (Look for a "reading glass" about two by four inches in a plastic frame.) Ask the kids to watch for the first unusual tree flowers, and, provided the trees are healthy and not in someone else's front yard, ask them to bring home a small sample for display and study. Keep the tree flowers in water after they have finished blooming and watch to see what comes next. For instance, maple flowers that were pollinated will begin to grow the typical winged fruit—the "keys"—that kids love to send spinning into the air.

If you start with the assumption that your trees do bloom, you'll see what you expect to see—tree flowers everywhere.

Tremors

*T*he San Francisco earthquake
occurred on April 18, 1906. There have been more horrifying
quakes in terms of devastation and loss of life, but the San
Francisco quake was pretty bad. It made itself felt over a
375,000-square-mile area. The fires that immediately followed it demolished the heart of the city. In all, close to five
square miles of San Francisco were lost. Although the Richter
scale had not been created at that time, scientists believe this
quake would have measured 8.25 or 8.3 on the scale. Now,
almost ninety years later, when you mention the San
Francisco quake, almost everyone knows which one you're
talking about. They will have seen the old pictures or heard
stories about it even though there was another major San
Francisco quake in 1989.

Ninety percent of the earthquakes in the United States occur
in California and Nevada, but there are plenty to go around.
Only a few, very small areas of the United States are free of
damaging quakes. An earthquake that occurred in Missouri
in 1811 was one of the worst ever to hit North America.
There were actually three quakes in that series, and the third,
on February 7, 1811, made itself felt as far away as
Washington, D.C., New Orleans, and Boston. In 1964 an
Alaskan earthquake centered near the head of Prince William
Sound sent shock waves eight hundred miles and set off a
tsunami that reached Japan, four thousand miles away.

In *Earthquake,* by Bryce Walker, the author says,

> The sheer physical magnitude of the Alaska earthquake was
> beyond comprehension. The initial seismic waves were so

powerful that they caused buildings to sway as far south as Seattle, Washington. Lengthening and weakening with distance, the radiating waves briefly lifted the ground beneath Houston, Texas, as much as four inches, and Cape Kennedy, Florida, two and a half inches. These movements were too gentle to be felt by the residents and were only revealed by later calculations based on tide levels. And as scientists reset their instruments and watched in fascination, the waves continued to circle the globe. For two weeks the entire planet vibrated like a great silent gong.

Was that some earthquake, or what?

There are about 120 earthquakes a year that hit 6 or more on the Richter scale. There is, on the average, a tremor somewhere on this planet every thirty seconds. They are as much a part of our world as the tides, our motion around the sun, and our weather. Right now, as a matter of fact, there is a good chance that someone, somewhere, is hanging on, waiting for the shaking to stop.

To the best of our present knowledge, there are three types of earthquakes: volcanic, plutonic, and tectonic. The volcanic is the least mysterious of all. Changes preceding and accompanying the eruption of a volcano set off earthquakes. Period. This is not hard to understand.

Plutonic quakes are probably the result of an eruption of molten rock onto the earth's crust. The molten rock solidifies and becomes part of the earth's upper crust, but it is so dense and heavy that it strains the surrounding crust. Any weaknesses in the crust may eventually give way under the stress—a plutonic quake. These two types constitute a very small part of the whole picture.

Tectonic quakes are the lead actors in the seismic arena. The present thinking is that the earth's crust is not a solid skin but a shifting, jostling group of immense plates that support the continents and ocean basins. They may travel at a rate of up to four inches a year, riding over a layer of softer molten rock. Four inches a year may not sound like much, but what we have here is an irresistible force meeting an immovable object. We're talking continents and whole ocean floors— ponderous, massive, inconceivably heavy juggernauts—rubbing shoulders or colliding head-on, sliding over each other or fracturing under pressure. Picture two of these giants (the plates under an ocean basin and a continent, for instance) getting hung up on each other, getting stuck so that their natural movements are not permitted any longer. Imagine the pressure between them building for years and years—fifty years is not very long when you're talking earthquakes. Then visualize the forces released when the inevitable happens, when one or the other slips or gives way.

It may be hard to believe, but it is possible that some quakes are blessings in disguise. The small quakes that ripple around the earth constantly probably release some pent-up plate energy in relatively harmless episodes. A tectonic process called subduction, whereby one plate slips under an opposing plate and goes down into the earth's molten interior to be melted and begin the whole cycle over again, may be part of an essential renewing process for the planet—the ultimate in recycling.

Much of the current research is focused on earthquake prediction. Many signs or symptoms have been observed before tremors occurred, ranging from extreme restlessness and uncharacteristic behavior in animals to the most delicate swelling of the earth's crust over a fault, but no one sign has always been present before every earthquake observed.

Quakes still strike with little or no warning that we can see and some strike where scientists would not have expected them to occur. Until that one infallible sign is isolated—if such a sign even exists—and until we can predict an earthquake at least as well as we can predict hurricanes or blizzards, we will have to cope with quakes that arrive unannounced.

If you find yourself in an earthquake, you should do the following:

- Stay indoors and get under something sturdy that will protect you from falling debris, such as a doorway frame or a solid desk or table. Flip over a sofa and crawl under that. Stay away from glass. Extinguish any source of flame.
- If you are outdoors, stay out and get as far away from buildings as you can. If you're in a car, drive off the bridge or overpass before you stop, and park out in the open.
- Remember that the most dangerous areas are those just outside buildings.
- Expect aftershocks. They don't always occur, but you should always expect them.
- When the shaking stops, get out of damaged buildings. Watch for live wires and gas leaks. Turn the gas or power off if you can do so safely.

Shortly after an earthquake occurs, there may be a tsunami (pronounced soo-nam-ee), a monster wave caused by the sudden, massive displacement of water, usually by earthquake movement, under water. Tsunamis are real killers. The inital displacement can occur near one shore and set off a wave that will crash onto another shore a thousand miles away, or it may occur unseen and unfelt on the ocean floor, resulting in a wave that spreads out like a ripple on a pond. In the open ocean, tsunamis may be only three feet tall and one hundred miles apart. A tsunami could pass under your boat at sea and not be noticed. But as it nears the coast, the rising land under the wave slows the bottom of the wave while the top continues to plunge ahead and build, turning into a monster. By the time our innocent-looking little three-footer smashes into a harbor somewhere, it could be one hundred feet tall. Imagine looking up at a wave one hundred feet tall. Sayonara.

So many people have been caught unaware by these killers that something has been done about it. There is now a Tsunami Warning System based in Honolulu that monitors the whole Pacific area constantly for any conditions that might create a tsunami. There will always be tsunamis, but by the time they reach land these days, their potential victims should have escaped to high ground.

Before we finish with earthquakes, we should take suitable notice of the Richter scale, which is a way scientists have of communicating with one another and us about the severity of an earthquake. Did you know that an increase of one whole number on the scale—from 4.0 to 5.0, for instance—means that the tremor registering 5.0 was actually ten times stronger than the one measuring 4? Each whole number represents a tenfold magnification.

The kids might like to make a cut-and-paste model of an earthquake. For $1.50 you can order a model of the 1989 Loma Prieta earthquake from the U. S. Geological Survey, Books and Open-File Reports Section, Box 2545, Denver, CO 80225. This model is for someone in the third or fourth grade and up, not the very young child.

Skunk Cabbage—Voodoo in the Marsh

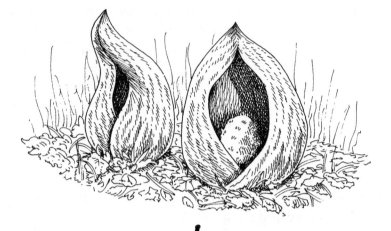

*I*t seems appropriate that April, which starts with April Fool's Day, is the time when skunk cabbage *(Symplocarpus foetidus)* appears. If ever there was a plant that looked like a practical joke, this is it.

To begin with, the first sign of a skunk cabbage's presence is a small, peaked hood that appears to have been carved out of mahogany and painted with thin yellow vertical stripes. This hood does not look plantlike in any way. It looks quite sinister, actually—the kind of thing you might wear to a voodoo ceremony in a larger size. Botanically speaking, it is a spathe—a modified leaf—that protects a little stalk inside called the spadix, which bears male or female flowers.

The plant converts starch stored in its root to achieve and maintain a temperature of 72 degrees Fahrenheit inside this little hood. When the day is bitterly cold, the skunk cabbage turns up the thermostat, and the air under the hood stays warm, 72 degrees. On warm, sunny days the conversion of starch to warmth slows down because less internally produced heat is needed. This heat enables the skunk cabbage to push up through the cold, hard ground of early spring in the first place and is an enticement to the flies and very early honeybees who serve as its pollinating agents. The heat may also make the famous skunk cabbage smell more noticeable to those pollinators who are searching for it.

Several days after the hood emerges, a tightly rolled green spear will appear right beside it, and this spear will shoot up and unfurl into a cluster of huge, bright green leaves that look as if they'd been plucked from some tropical-theme wallpaper. If it is a warm spring and you live within walking distance of a skunk cabbage, it will pay for you to stroll by the bog every twenty-four hours and see what a difference a day makes. Kids appreciate fast action, and a skunk cabbage grows like green lightning when the weather is right.

By the time the leaves are fully opened, the hood will have shrunk and collapsed and almost disappeared, like the Wicked Witch of the West when Dorothy's pail of water hit her.

Crush a skunk cabbage leaf in your hand. The aroma is definitely skunky. Once you have gotten a good whiff, you will understand why these plants are pollinated by flies. They must be attracted by the odor. It smells like carrion, something that's been dead for a long time. (The kids may say "Yuck!" but they probably won't mean it. At a certain age yucky things are immensely appealing.) The smell will wash off, fortunately, if you dip your hand in the creek or the pond.

When you look across a bog at this time of year and see clusters of gorgeous green leaves held high above the muck, you're probably looking at skunk cabbage.

The Lion Walks Tonight

·   ☆   ✳   ○   ◎   ◎
5   4   3   2   1   0 magnitude

*T*he Lion is easy to spot in the April sky because he strides through a relatively uncrowded area. He is about four-fifths of the way up the sky between the eastern horizon and the zenith (that imaginary spot directly over your head). When you're looking for him, face east and then just let your eyes drift up until they reach a magnificent white star high in the sky. That'll be Regulus, and it marks one of the Lion's forepaws. A little north of Regulus, can you see the stars that set off his proudly arched neck and his head? Working back toward the east, look for the stars that outline his hindquarters, tail, and rear legs.

Even after we have located some constellations, we have struggled in vain to "see" the animal or person the constellation was named for. We love Cassiopeia, but Cassie looks to us like a big *M* or *W* or *3*, depending on the season, and we cannot honestly say we see a queen or her chair up there. But with the Lion, we do see a lion.

Regulus is a first magnitude star. Denebola, at the tip of the Lion's tail, is also very bright, a second magnitude star. I will resist the impulse to call it a "taillight."

Because the Lion walks the ecliptic, the pathway across the sky followed by the planets, you may sometimes see an even more brilliant "star" where you didn't expect to see one—under his paws, perhaps. For more information on planets, turn to *June*.

We have a very nice grouping in the western sky around nine in the evening, late in the month. The Twins (Gemini—see *March*) prance along arm in arm just above the western horizon; the Little Dog (Canis Minor) follows them faithfully; and the Lion (Leo), big, bold, and beautiful, has swung around to the spot just southwest of the zenith and is striding down the sky toward them.

May

Frog and Toad Night—Tadpoles Resulting

At least once every spring there will be a long, soft day of rain followed by a warm, moist night. When the temperature stays high enough, long enough, and the ground becomes saturated—when conditions are exactly right—there will be what we call a Frog and Toad Night.

You'll know it when you see it. You'll be driving down some country or suburban road, perhaps a road that separates a wooded area from a swamp or a creek, and you will begin to notice dozens and dozens of toads and frogs hopping erratically across the gleaming pavement, spotlighted by your car headlights. Some will continue to hop as you approach. Others, still sluggish after months of hibernation or dazzled by the brilliance of your headlights, will stop and sit there in the road like tiny stone statues.

This mass migration, triggered by subtle seasonal signals, and warmth and moisture, is the start of the courtship and breeding season for many species of toads and frogs. Some frogs spend the winter buried in the mud at the bottom of a pond, but many frogs and toads hibernate in a burrow or deep cranny in a wooded area. Now courtship songs must be sung, the fertilization of eggs must take place, and those eggs must be laid in water. So it's everyone into the pool—or into the slow-moving river or the swamp or even the ditch.

If you discover that a Frog and Toad Night is going on, why not let the kids come out and watch? Bundle everyone up (if possible, see that each child is wearing something white, for safety's sake) and hand out flashlights. Warn the kids not to put their hands in their mouth, eyes, or nose if they have touched a toad. Some of these little animals, if frightened or handled roughly, release a fluid that is irritating to mucous membranes. This fluid will not cause warts—I don't care what Aunt Mary said—but in the mouth, it makes a person uncomfortable for a while.

If the kids are old enough to handle frogs and toads gently, let them catch a few specimens each and try to identify them. There are plenty of amphibian guides on the market; my personal favorite is described at the end of this section.

The kids will discover, as they go frog-catching, that most frogs can jump farther and faster than most toads and even than most children. There will be a good deal of falling down and giggling, and muddiness on everything and everyone, but twenty years from now, when the kids get together, maybe they will reminisce about the night you took them all out frogging.

When Frog and Toad Night is over and all the eggs have been deposited in water, the adult frogs and toads go on about their business, taking up a summer residence in the woods, someone's garden, a meadow, or the margin of a pond.

The eggs—those that haven't been eaten by other pond inhabitants—will hatch into tadpoles in a remarkably short time, a matter of days in some cases. If you take everyone back to the pond on a warm, sunny day later in May or in early June, you should see swarms of squiggly little tadpoles in the shallow water. The kids will want to take some home, of course, Why not? Seeing the tadpoles turn into tiny toads and frogs is fascinating, and the care they require at this stage is minimal. Take as much pond water home with you as you can, to start them out in, and fill another little bucket or jar with aquatic plants and water to serve as your tadpole larder.

Many a tadpole has been raised successfully in a large mayonnaise jar. Figure that a one-gallon jar will accommodate five or six tadpoles. A small, vacant aquarium tank is even better than a jar. Place them where they will get lots of light but no direct sun. Let me say that again: *no direct sun,* or you could end up with poached tadpoles by evening.

At this stage tadpoles are vegetarians. A small helping of pond vegetation served once a day will feed a jarful. Remove any leftovers before feeding again, in the interests of cleanliness. If there are no leftovers, give them more next time. If you run out of pond plants temporarily, give them a freshly boiled lettuce or spinach leaf instead. One or two experts recommend using cornmeal. I have never tried that. I'm not sure how you would get the leftover cornmeal out in order to keep the water fresh.

The tadpoles will spend from several weeks to one or more years as tadpoles, depending on their species. (Bullfrogs are late bloomers who may take a year or more to fully mature. Bullfrog tads are quite large by the time they're ready to make the change to frog—too large for a mayonnaise jar. You had better select fairly small tads, all about the same size.)

Most tads make the transition to miniature frogs or toads in a matter of weeks. Since you won't know what species you're raising or when they hatched, you can't know what timetable they're on. It is a good idea to check them for developmental changes every day. Changes sometimes occur with amazing speed, and not always in the order you would have expected. Think of it as waiting to find the solution to a mystery or unwrapping very small surprise packages.

The word *amphibian* used to describe frogs and toads comes from the Greek words meaning "life" and "on both sides." The basic word therefore means "living on both sides," and they do. They start life in the water as aquatic animals, breathing through gills. When they mature from tadpoles into tiny frogs and toads, they become lung breathers. This process is called "metamorphosis," another fifty-cent word from the Greek meaning "a change in form," and that certainly describes what happens to tadpoles.

When you see definite signs that your tadpoles are becoming tiny frogs and toads (minuscule legs appear, and the tail shortens) and notice that they are constantly coming up to the surface to breathe, put into the jar a bit of wood or buoyant plastic, something flat that will float. They must have something they can climb out on so they can get a breath of air. Remember, they are becoming lung breathers like you and me, and, just like you and me, they need to be able to haul out and rest or they will drown. Try offering them a bit of commercially prepared, canned dog food, the kind that is all meat, if possible, on the end of a broomstraw. Wave it around, wiggle it, tease them. Make your morsel look as it if were alive and stupid—coming that close to a budding frog.

When the transformation is complete, you will have a raftful of miniature hoppers. By now you may be quite fond of them; they have a definite perky charm. You can hold a sort of graduation ceremony back at the pond and send your little guests on their way to adulthood, or if one of the kids is interested, you can create a terrarium-with-pool for the toads and go into live-insect feeding, or set up a frog aquarium. (Turn to *November* for terrarium instructions.) Someone will have to research your particular species of frog to find out what it requires for good health. Don't discourage or disparage an abiding interest in frogs or toads or other small creatures. These animals can be quite interesting and even beautiful, in their own way.

Incidentally, if you put your houseplants out on the porch for the summer (an excellent idea), try to interest a toad in spending his summer out there with them. Provide a shady corner where he will not be disturbed, a pie plate full of water, and a daily spritzing; he will settle down blissfully and patrol the porch for insects. If you garden outdoors, let the grass under the outdoor spigot get nice and long, and wet it down every day or so. Toads will appreciate this, and you will appreciate their work in your garden. You will have entered a "symbiotic" relationship (from the Greek *sym* meaning "with" or "together," and *bio* meaning "to live"). You will be two dissimilar organisms living together in a mutually beneficial way.

Ask the kids if they can think of any other symbiotic relationships they might be part of. Do they have a pet, a dog or a cat?

It may not be a symbiotic relationship in the strictest scientific sense of the word, but it is an exchange of unconditional love and companionship for food, shelter, and care. That's probably one of my favorite symbiotic things.

IF YOU WOULD LIKE TO ATTRACT ORIOLES THIS SUMMER, CUT A SWEET, JUICY ORANGE IN HALF, RUN A PIECE OF STRING THROUGH THE CENTER OF EACH HALF, AND HANG THE HALVES ON THE BRANCHES OF A TREE WHERE THEY WILL BE SEEN BY ANY BIRDS FLYING THROUGH YOUR YARD. DO NOT WAIT UNTIL YOU SEE ORIOLES TO HANG OUT AN ORANGE. PUT IT OUT THERE, AND IF THERE ARE ORIOLES IN YOUR TERRITORY, THEY'LL SHOW UP. YOU WILL LOOK OUT THE WINDOW SOME MORNING AND SEE A BRILLIANT BLACK-AND-ORANGE BIRD HANGING UPSIDE DOWN ON YOUR ORANGE, GETTING ITS JUICE FIX FOR THE DAY. WHEN THE FRUIT HAS BEEN PICKED CLEAN, TAKE IT DOWN, CUT A NEW LENGTH OF STRING AND A NEW ORANGE, AND PUT IT UP AGAIN! AND IF, IN THE MONTH OF MAY, YOU SLIP SEVERAL FIVE-INCH PIECES OF COTTON STRING OR WOOL YARN (NO MAN-MADE FIBERS, PLEASE) THROUGH THE STRING GOING THROUGH THE ORANGE HALF, SOMEONE WILL EVENTUALLY TAKE THAT STRING HOME TO INCLUDE IN A NEST. ACT ON FAITH. PUT THOSE ORANGE HALVES OUT AND EXPECT ORIOLES.

Honeybees and Their Dance of the Flowers

Next time you pass a blooming apple tree on a warm, sunny day, stop and listen. The tree hums. Can you hear it?

Actually, the tree isn't humming, of course—hundreds of honeybees are. They are working over the tree in search of nectar and, coincidentally, are cross-pollinating the tree so that it will produce a good crop.

No need for alarm. It has been our experience that most "bee" stings were actually delivered by wasps or hornets. Honeybees look like cinnamon-colored cigars—short and chubby, with darker stripes around their abdomens. Their bodies are slightly fuzzy. Wasps have slender, pointed, smooth bodies, and their abdomens are quite noticeably joined to the rest of the body by a thin stalk. Bee wings are short and broad. Wasp wings are longer and more elegant looking.

Bees will not normally bother you unless you appear to be threatening them or, even more important, threatening their hive. Wasps and hornets seem to have shorter fuses. The African bees—the "angry" bees you have heard about—have become a real problem in South America. People in the United States are working on ways to control them. It isn't so much that these bees are really "angry" all the time or have particularly poisonous venom. It's that they tend to get angry more quickly; they are more tenacious about pursuing someone they feel threatened by, and once they're irritated, they seem to attack in far greater numbers. If these bees become established in the United States, we will have to find some selective way of coping with them or getting rid of them—and just them. Even if we wanted to and had the means to do it, killing off all the bees in this country to get rid of the African bees is out of the question. Over fifty agricultural crops in the United States depend on bees as their primary pollinators.

A honeybee is a most effective pollinator because she is "loyal." She has a certain degree of flower fidelity, and as a result, if you captured a working honeybee and removed all the pollen she was carrying, chances are it would all be from the same species of flower. That is why apiarists can sell us "clover honey" and "orange blossom honey." While the bee is gathering nectar up front, her rear legs are being dusted with pollen from the blossom she is resting on, and they are also depositing pollen from the blossom she just left. With most other insects, it's apple blossoms now and clover two minutes later, and dandelions five minutes after that. If you were an apple grower, you would not consider this a big help. Orchardists encourage flower fidelity by mowing down all the other tantalizing flowers near their orchards just before their fruit trees bloom.

There is some disagreement as to just how far a bee will travel to load up on nectar, but the preponderance of opinion seems to set a limit of two miles. A worker bee may produce just a thimbleful of honey during her whole hardworking career. That spoonful of honey on your toast represents a lot of wingbeats.

Experiments have shown that honeybees dance messages for the other bees in their hives, giving exact information about what flowers are in bloom, the quality and quantity of the nectar, the time of day when the nectar is most heavily pro-duced, the flowers' location, and even how much effort it will take to gather nectar from them and bring it home (head winds, and so forth). One "dance" consists of figure-eight movements on the inside wall of the hive, in the dark, accompanied by significant body wigwagging, as if the bee were using her body as a semaphore. Other worker bees gather around the dancer, touching her frequently. Valuable information is brought back to the hive and disseminated to all its members as rapidly as possible. Twenty different dances have been observed and recorded, but to date only a few have been decoded or interpreted.

You may have heard about swarms of bees and find the idea of thousands of bees, all flying together or collecting in a mass, pretty scary. Swarming bees are just looking for a new home; that's all they and their queen are interested in. If you discover a swarm in your yard someday, please don't panic or try to destroy it. Call your local police station; they will usually know who to contact for you. If they don't, call your university extension service or beekeepers' association. Someone will come and help.

Not so long ago every farm had its hives of bees, and there was a folk tradition that when someone in the family died, a member of the family had to go down to the hive and tell the bees. People took this custom very seriously and did inform the hive. In some areas, hives were also decorated or draped with a bit of black cloth following a family death. There seems to have been an almost mystical quality to the relationship between old-time beekeepers and their bees.

For a bee project, why not buy some honey still in the comb at your local health food store. Let those kids who are old enough to chew gum, chew the comb until all the honey is gone and they are left with a small ball of pure white wax. When it is at body temperature, they can work with this as if it were modeling clay. You could also make some honeycomb candles. You can buy thin sheets of comb for about $1.00

each, and wicking for pennies per candle, at a good craft and art supply store. Lay a sheet of comb on a clean, dry tabletop. Cut a length of wick about half an inch longer than the short side of the sheet. Place the wick right on a short edge of the sheet and press it gently into the wax so it will stay put. Now roll the comb up like a jelly roll. All the kids—even the little ones—can safely do this. When your candle is finished, press the loose edge into the side of the candle very gently, with the blunt end of a ballpoint pen or your fingernail, in a dozen places so it will look neatly finished. Squeeze the bottom of the candle, working around and around with your fingers, until it will fit into your candle holder. Light up. As the candle burns, the wax below the flame will glow and a subtle, sweet honey scent will float in the air. If this isn't the essence of summer—light, warmth, and sweetness—I don't know what is.

These candles make very nice gifts. The kids might like to make some for a favorite teacher or someone in the family who entertains a lot. Wrap the candles in paper or clear wrap, and store them in a cool, dry spot. In wintertime they will bring back summer memories.

Does a Robin See, Hear, or Feel His Dinner Coming?

*D*id you ever wonder how a robin knows where to peck to get its worm? Did it perhaps hear a faint rumble as the earthworm tunneled through your garden, or were those tunneling vibrations picked up by the robin's scaly little feet? Those two theories have been around for a long time. The latest opinion—and it sounds strange even to me—is that earthworms come to the surface and then pause to rest from their labors, with their stubby little heads poking out of the ground. And while they're just hanging out, as it were, the robins, who have exceptional eyesight, spot them and snatch them. That would explain why a robin will pause with its head tilted to one side for a moment before diving for a worm. It sees the worm and is sizing up the situation carefully, because it knows it won't get a second shot.

I favor this third theory, bizarre as it may seem, because I spent some time recently watching a robin hunting for and eating its breakfast, and the evidence forced me to come to the following conclusions: It is improbable that a robin feels vibration through its feet because it is frequently standing on grass and, under that, a layer of fine litter—dead grass clippings, tiny pebbles, old leaves, and so forth. It is unlikely that hearing alone guides the robin, because it acts exactly the way it behaves going after worms (hop along, pause with head on one side, snatch!) when it's picking bugs off buttercups. A bug taking its ease on a buttercup stem is not making a racket or creating a lot of commotion. So by the process of elimination, I'd say the robin uses its eyesight more than its hearing or the sensitivity of its feet, and the third theory must come closer to the truth than the other two.

It will take only five minutes for the kids to conduct their own experiment on this subject. Robins spend most of their time hunting for food during this season, so locating a robin or two and figuring out how they are getting their worms shouldn't take too long. And it's an easy introduction to the naturalist's habit of quietly observing and then coming to the conclusion that seems most likely to him. Maybe one of your children will notice something no one else has noticed or will come up with an explanation no one else has thought of.

What Can You Count On? The North Star

Now that you have a new wind vane in the backyard (see *March*) and it's swinging around, nosing into the early morning breeze like an excited young hound, someone may raise the question: "What direction is that, anyway?"

Good question, because it matters. A wind from the southwest could mean "Get out the suntan lotion and the beach towels," but a wind from the southeast might mean "Take in the lawn furniture and get out the slickers!" How does a person who doesn't know which direction is which go about finding out without a compass?

Someone will immediately suggest the rising and setting sun, east and west. This shows that the kids are still with you and are thinking, but you will have to break it to them that the sun appears to rise at different points on the horizon at different seasons, which gives you a movable east and also a movable west. If someone challenges this unsettling concept, ask him or her to draw a little sketch of the horizon that is seen out a window, provided it's a window from which you can actually see the sun set or rise. Now ask him or her to date it and make a mark where the sun set or rose that day. There is bound to be some landmark—a big tree, a smokestack, or a hilltop—that will serve as a reference point for the sun's posi-

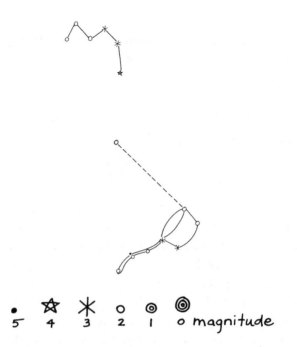

tion. It is important to warn the kids not to stare directly at the setting or rising sun. Not ever. They can look to one side of it, and for our purposes that will be close enough. If the child is very young, it would be safer and just as effective to let him or her make a small chalk mark on the bedroom wall where the first sunbeam of the day lands or the last rays of the setting sun fade away. Let's assume that we're doing this on May 1 and that the solstice comes on June 21 this year. Tape the little sketch to the window and on the solstice ask the child to make another mark on the sketch to indicate where the sun set or rose that day, or to look for the May 1 chalk mark. *Caramba!* What's going on here? Fifty-two days later, check the sun's position again. It should be back almost exactly where it was on May 1. But we're not done yet. Leave the sketch or chalk mark up, and just before Christmas check one last time. Whoa! You can almost feel the earth tilting beneath your feet as you look at how far south the sun has traveled since August 12. If you would like to demonstrate why the earth and sun appear to go swinging wildly through space like this, go to *September* for instructions on making a model of the seasonal dance of the earth and sun.

Since the places where the sun rises and sets—solar east and west, if you will—are influenced by the seasons, we need something else, something that will not move no matter what the time of year. Many people believe that moss grows only on the northern side of trees. Find yourself a mossy tree, they say, and there you are! But there are trees with moss growing on their eastern, southern, and western sides, because of the lay of the land around them or nearby bogs or rivers. How about the North Star, sometimes called the Pole (or pole) star, or Polaris? It is always close enough to due north to be your trusted guide. (Even the North Star has undergone some changes over thousands of years, but we don't have to worry about that. For this generation and many more to follow, the North Star will remain the North Star.)

In May the Big Dipper will be almost over your head, near the zenith (the point in the sky directly over the observer). The dipper will appear to be turned upside down, emptying its contents down the side of the sky. The two stars outlining the side of the dipper bowl opposite the handle are called the Pointer Stars, because they always point to the North Star. Begin with the star highest in the sky, the one marking the bottom corner of the dipper bowl (remember that the bowl is upside down right now). Come down the side of the dipper through the Pointer Star marking the top of the dipper bowl, opposite the handle. Now extend that line until you hit a star about halfway down the sky toward the horizon—the North Star. No matter what position the Big Dipper is in—upside down or right side up—and no matter what time of year it is, those two Pointer Stars will point to the North Star. You can depend on it. The rest is easy. When you are facing north, south is behind you, east is on your right, and west is on your left.

You can never tell when knowing how to find north at night might come in handy. If you were lost out on the water or in the woods, it could be a useful piece of information to have.

Did you know that all the stars overhead circle around the North Star as the evening and the seasons go by? It is our only celestial constant.

Before you go in tonight, take a stick and scratch a deep N on the ground just to the north of the new vane.

June

The Dawn Chorus

*T*here is a phenomenon—
"something that impresses the observer as extraordinary, a remarkable happening"—that occurs every day during the months of May and June, before the sun comes up. It is the Dawn Chorus, a brief period of time when all the birds in an area sing together. It sounds as if every bird feels compelled to let the others know that it, too, has made it safely through the night and is celebrating.

This morning the first bird sang a few bars in the cool darkness at 4:33 A.M. By 4:35 a sprinkling of birds all over the lot had joined in—a trill from deep in the honeysuckle, a strident call repeated several times from the top of one of the old pines. With every passing minute from then on, more singers joined in until by 4:43 we were surrounded by a cloud of bird song. It became impossible to sort out the individual singers.

There was just a rising swell of bird music in the air. This was not a subtle experience, not a soft communal chirping that one could easily overlook. It was loud and jubilant. Standing outdoors, you felt as if you were at the bottom of a deep well of music.

By 5:03 the song was ending. The singers were starting to go about their business of catching the early worm. By 5:17 the singing had diminished to the short solos that go on all day. At 5:23 the sun came up on a world that had already heard its wake-up call.

If you get up to listen to the Dawn Chorus just once, it is a good idea to stay with it to the end. You need the contrast, from that first note in semidarkness through the magnificent crescendo and back down to the last few bars in the clear brightness of dawn, to enjoy the sheer volume and beauty of the chorus.

When you hear all the birds in your yard singing, you will hardly believe how many there are. We feed the birds all year and have been casual bird-watchers for decades, but every time I listen to the Dawn Chorus, I know we've missed more birds than we saw or heard during the day.

The smallest children may not be ready to appreciate the chorus, just as they do not get a lot out of some human music that adults love. Ask the older kids if they would like to experience this with you, then set out the doughnuts and cold milk or orange juice and muffins, and eat, drink, and be merry while you listen to the Dawn Chorus.

Our Nearest Neighbor, the Moon

*T*he moon and June have long
been linked in our minds as a particularly compatible and
potent combination. Well, June moons are nice, but how
about a February moon flooding snowfields with clear silver?
Or an October moon rising over the edge of the world like a
great golden balloon? Or a March moon gliding serenely
above a sky filled with tattered, wind-whipped clouds? The
truth is, every month's moon is beautiful.

The moon is our nearest neighbor, our satellite, and we are
well aware of her control over our tides. For thousands of
years man has debated whether or not the moon also has an
influence on us and our crops. It seems to me that anything
powerful enough to lift oceans—how much would just one
square mile of ocean weigh?—might at least tug at other ener-
gies, too. Influence between the earth and the moon is not a
one-way street. The gravitational pull of the earth forces the
moon to go through one complete rotation every month, so
the moon always presents the same face to the earth. We had
to go out into space and loop around behind it to discover
what its back side looked like. Very much like the front side,
as I understand it.

The moon appears to rise in the east and set in the west.
Each day it rises approximately fifty minutes later than it did
the day before. It goes through seven stages, or phases, every
29½ days.

The new moon appears in our daytime sky. The sun is shin-
ing on the side of the moon away from us, and since it has no
light of its own, the side of the moon toward us is dark and

does not appear to shine. You have to look hard to see it—a pale ghost moon.

A moon becoming more full is called a waxing moon. At the waxing crescent stage, the moon rises later than the sun and sets during the early evening.

The first quarter is the half-moon stage. It gets up around noon and disappears in the middle of the night. Well, every family has someone like that in its midst.

The gibbous moon (would I make a word like that up?) rises late in the day and sets in the small hours of the morning. It appears to be an almost full moon. (The g in gibbous is pronounced as if it were the g in gibbon, the ape, not the g in giant.)

The full moon rises early in the evening and sets at sunrise. Although all of our side of the moon is in this phase, it may not be the best time to study the moon. There are no profile shadows on its face to make for interesting contrasts. It is like taking pictures at noon—too much light washes the details out. Try studying the moon through 7×50 binoculars when it's waning or waxing. The craters and seas are astonishingly clear, and those on the line between light and shadow are dramatically highlighted.

Since the moon has no protective atmospheric barrier, it has probably been hit often and hit hard by asteroids and comets. It is thought that the craters were formed when bits and pieces of interstellar debris slammed into the moon. We know now that the moon's "seas"—maria—were never saltwater seas. They may have been created by floods of lava soon after the moon was formed, or they may have been the result of asteroid or comet impact so devastating that areas of the moon's surface melted. Solid rock became a liquid for a while and acted like a liquid; it left a liquidlike print on the moon's surface for us to puzzle over.

The last quarter moon—a waning or declining moon—rises around midnight and sets around noon.

The waning crescent rises before sunrise and sets in mid- or late afternoon. And shortly after that we begin all over again with the new moon, which rises approximately when the sun does.

One foolproof way to know whether you are looking at a waning or waxing moon is to compare it to a C or D. A D-shaped crescent—D for daring—is waxing or growing. A C-shaped crescent—C for coy—is waning or disappearing. H. A. Rey suggests this memory aid in his book *The Stars,* and I've found it helpful—the tip and the book.

If it should rain one June afternoon and the kids get restless, suggest that they set up a sun-moon-earth display to dazzle Grandma with when she comes to Sunday dinner.

They will need one grapefruit, four oranges, four Ping-Pong balls, one felt-tipped black marker (*not* waterproof), and lots of space.

Unless you're laying this out to some sort of scale on a golf course, you're going to have to ignore real distances and sizes. The earth's diameter is just under 8,000 miles. The moon's diameter is about 2,160 miles. The sun's diameter is 865,000 miles. If we used a scale of 1 inch to represent 1,000 miles, our sun would be 865 inches (or a little over 72 feet) across, the earth would be 8 inches across, and the moon would be just over 2 inches across. You can see the problem here. It gets worse. The sun is 93 million miles from the earth. I'm not even going to try to translate that into feet and inches. Once you have explained that we are going to ignore actual sizes and distances, you can proceed with a clear conscience.

Have someone color half of each Ping-Pong ball black with the marker.

Put the grapefruit, which will represent our sun, in the middle of the available space. Place the oranges, which will represent our earth as it orbits, so they form an arc that is about $\frac{1}{12}$ of a big imaginary circle around the sun.

Place one Ping-Pong ball close to the first orange, between it and the sun. Place a second ball in line with the oranges, to the left of the second orange. Place a third ball on the far side of the third orange so that the orange stands between the Ping-Pong ball and the grapefruit. The fourth ball will go in line with the oranges, to the right of the fourth orange. Remember that the light side of each Ping-Pong ball must always face the sun since the moon gives off no light of its own.

If you were standing on the earth as it revolved, you would see only the shadowed side of the moon in the first example, which would mean you were experiencing a new moon, right? The second set of ball and orange represents a waxing moon or quarter moon situation. You would see a moon half in shadow and half in light, from the side. The third set illustrates a full moon. The lighted side of the ball faces the earth as well as the sun. The fourth set demonstrates a fourth quarter placement—we see the moon half lighted and half in shadow, from the side—a waning moon.

You might suggest that the kids study the first and third placements for a minute to see if they can guess what fairly unusual occurrences may happen when the moon, earth, and sun are in those positions. The answer is a lunar and a solar eclipse. When the moon comes exactly between the sun and the earth, the moon blots out the sun and briefly throws its own shadow over part of the earth. That is a solar eclipse. When the earth comes exactly between the sun and the moon, and throws its shadow over the full moon, that is a lunar eclipse. Because the moon's orbit is not exactly on the same plane as the earth's, we do not have a lunar eclipse with every full moon or a solar eclipse with every new moon. Eclipses are regular and predictable, though.

You might also discuss with the kids what effect a solar or lunar eclipse might have had on a primitive family. How would they have reacted, not knowing about eclipses, if sudden darkness occurred in the middle of the day? How would they have felt if they saw a full moon being swallowed up right before their eyes in a matter of minutes? What explanations might have occurred to them? Wouldn't it have looked to them as if something or somebody were eating the moon? It sure would, and many myths and folk stories explain the event just that way.

Now if Grandma isn't dazzled by all this, send her home without dessert.

Before you wash off those Ping-Pong balls, try playing a game of Ping-Pong with them still half black and half white. Now you see them, now you don't. It sure adds an element of chance to the game, doesn't it?

Firefly Night-Lights

There is no nicer night-light in this world than a jelly jar full of fireflies. I wonder how many little kids have been lighted to sleep this way through the years.

To acquire a firefly night-light, one must first start with a leisurely after-dinner firefly hunt. It takes time to learn the ways of fireflies, and your eyes must become accustomed to the deepening darkness. It also takes a patient parent or two to help someone small whose reflexes are not very quick because she's tired.

Give everyone his or her own quart-size plastic ice cream carton or pint-size refrigerator container with a lid for catching. Plastic is a lot safer than glass when everyone is running around, bumping into everyone else, and giggling. When you have caught a firefly in the carton, its glow will show through, never fear. It will remind you of Tinker Bell's light in *Peter Pan.*

Transfer each firefly to a glass jar held by someone who is just standing there—the Keeper of the Lights, we'll call him.

Fireflies (they're not really flies but members of a beetle family) are harder to catch than you might think. They appear to be just floating along or waiting to be scooped up, but they can move quite rapidly when they have to. The ones in the grass or on the road or driveway are usually female. Many of them are wingless. Those drifting through the treetops or six feet over the lawn are usually males. The light flashing is either an invitation to mate or the response to an invitation.

When each child has captured three or four beetles, add a few leaves or sprigs of grass to each jar, a bit of old, moist wood perhaps, and a drop or two of water. Then puncture the jar lid with a very slender nail in several places or cover the jar with clear wrap secured with a rubber band, and punch air holes in the wrap very carefully with a needle.

While you are all out there pursuing fireflies, someone will ask you how they do that—make their own light inside their bodies.

The light is what you might call a cold light. It reminds me of pale blue or green neon light. Almost all of the energy put into the firefly's flash results in light, whereas 75 percent to 90 percent of the energy in a lighted electric bulb is producing heat, not light. Anyone who has touched an electric light bulb that has been on for a while knows how true that is. The cool light is called "bioluminescence." It is caused by a heatless chemical reaction. The firefly combines oxygen with a substance called luciferin, which produces this cool green light when an enzyme called luciferase is present. When the flash impulse stops, the chemical ingredients in the lighting system go back to the way they were until the time comes for the next flash. The timing for the flashing is determined by the beetle's species and the temperature. You will notice that on cool evenings there are very few flashes to be seen, but on hot nights there is a whole lot of flashing going on.

The next morning, before you go to work, set the fireflies free. The kids are likely to forget in the bright light of morning.

There are fireflies in warmer climates that give off a great deal of light. It is said that four of them together can produce enough light to read a newspaper by. And once in a while all the fireflies in an area will flash on and flash off simultaneously. Now that would be something to see.

Twister!

*T*here are very few natural events that have the fascination for us of a tornado. Check it out the next time there are pictures of one on the evening news. The kids will look up from the comics and watch. The chef will come out of the kitchen to have a look. Grandma will hit SAVE on the computer and turn around to see them. No one can ignore a tornado.

Tornadoes sometimes occur when a deep layer of cold, dry air overrides a layer of warm, moist air. That is a highly unstable situation because hot air tends to rise and cool air to fall. Something is bound to happen, but that something is not always a tornado. Thunderstorms or hailstorms may result instead, or they may precede or accompany tornadoes. And not all funnel clouds touch down to earth and become tornadoes. When they do, they may leap about like elephantine ballerinas or plow straight across the face of the land like monster bulldozers. There is no sure way to predict which way they'll go, either, but they do travel from southwest to northeast about 85 percent of the time.

The destructive clout of a tornado is a combination of winds that may hit 250 to 300 miles an hour and an incredibly rapid drop in barometric pressure. It is hard to say which does the most damage. The original theory was that when the barometric pressure outside a house dropped several inches in a few seconds, the house exploded because the greater pressure inside it ballooned the walls and popped the roof. This would explain why you see so many roofless houses after a tornado. Now, however, many meteorologists believe that the tornado winds rip a house apart and toss it around, independent of the drop in pressure. I guess that if your house ends up spread all over town, it doesn't matter a whole lot which did the greatest damage—the wind or the drop in pressure.

A tornado in contact with the ground is a dark funnel because its walls are filled with debris. It is acting like a giant vacuum cleaner. Remember Dorothy and Toto? Well, that's what it's like.

The damage done by tornadoes can be awe-inspiring—cars flattened into sheets of metal, barns lifted and set down a quarter mile away—and it can be unexpectedly whimsical. Tornadoes have driven straws through oak planks, and two-by-fours through half-inch steel plates. These cases defy every fact we know about the relative strengths of straw, oak, pine, and steel, so scientists conjecture that, for a fraction of a second, under the impact of wildly fluctuating barometric pressure and incredible wind force, the molecular structures of the oak and steel were actually temporarily changed.

When they are in contact with the ground, most tornadoes cut a swath about three hundred to four hundred yards wide and travel about twenty-five to forty miles an hour. The average life expectancy of a tornado is ten minutes (that can fluctuate widely, too), and it might cover ten miles or more.

If you are in a building when a tornado hits, remember that the ground floor and basement are the safest locations. Stay in small-area rooms with lots of supporting walls and pipes—a stairwell, an inside hall, a bathroom, or a closet. Get under the pool table or turn the sofa over and get under that. Stay away from windows. The glass will shatter and turn into razorlike projectiles. If there are windows everywhere, protect yourself with a blanket or heavy coat.

If you are caught out in the open and spot a tornado headed your way but still some distance off, don't try to outrun it.

Make a sharp turn to the left or right, and make haste! Take off! Do not stop to admire that tornado. If it leapfrogs around, it could land on you. Keep moving until the tornado has left.

If the twister is too close for you to get away safely, find a ditch and lie down in it. If you can't find a ditch, ravine, or culvert, lie under your car and pray. Don't sit the storm out in your car unless that car is traveling at right angles to the storm at about eighty miles an hour. Cars are not tornado-proof. A mobile home is even more vulnerable.

A *tornado watch* indicates that conditions exist that may spawn a tornado. Listen up and check the sky every few minutes.

A *tornado warning* means that a tornado has actually been sighted in the area covered by the warning. If you are in that area, figure that it's coming your way and act accordingly. Until you hear the all-clear on your radio, stay under cover or right beside cover. Remember that tornadoes can travel as fast as or faster than most car traffic.

If there is a tornado watch on at night and you suddenly hear something like a freight train coming at you, head for the basement as fast as you can, because that freight train is a tornado. That's what they sound like—a freight train with a high-pitched scream.

Discuss tornadoes with the kids as casually and lightly as possible while still getting your points across about what to do if . . . The chances are they'll never need this information, but if they do, they'll need it right then.

To lighten up a kind of scary subject, get a gadget called the Tornado Tube; it retails at about $2.50 and can be found at places such as your nearest Audubon center or nature store. You use the tube to connect two plastic bottles—ordinary two-liter soda bottles are fine. Then, following the very simple directions, you create a swirling, twisting miniature tornado, in water, in one of the bottles. You can even add glitter or food dye to enhance the special effects. The kids will love it. If you can't find a tube locally, write Tornado Tube, 26 Dearborn Street, Salem, MA 01970.

To the Sea, to the Sea, to the Beautiful Sea

$\mathcal{S}$ooner or later we all end up at the beach. Sometimes it looks as if we all picked the same day to go there. If you live anywhere near the sea, you know there is a magnetic pull toward salt water that is particularly strong on weekends. Scientists have never been able to confirm the existence of this force, but it's there all right. You come out the front door headed for a neighborhood park, everyone gets in the car, and before you know it, the dog is getting sick in the backseat and the parking lot attendant is asking you for $10.00 and reminding you that the beach closes at 9 P.M. on Sundays. How much more proof do you need?

Unfortunately, sometimes there are hazardous conditions even at the beach. Undertow is probably what springs to mind first.

Not everything that is called an undertow is the genuine article. People will tell you they were almost pulled under and out to sea by an undertow at this or that beach when all they experienced was the natural backwash of spent waves. All that water comes pounding onto the beach and stops. Now it

has to go back, because the beach slopes down to the sea. On a steep beach it flows back very rapidly and with real force. That can be alarming if you're not prepared for it; it feels as if the water is pulling your feet out from under you. But feeling sucked seaward by water several inches deep is not an undertow or even the sign of an undertow. The worst that can happen under those circumstances is that you sit down suddenly and get chucked under the chin by the next incoming wave.

A real undertow is a swift, strong, localized current headed out to sea. This current is almost impossible to fight. You may swim hard toward shore, really stroking, and still find yourself getting farther and farther away from the beach. Once you understand what causes the undertow, you'll know what to do. If there are a great many waves coming in fast and breaking on an underwater sandbar at some distance from the waterline, you can actually have a buildup of water on the shore side of the bar. More water is being brought in than can rapidly get out. The "excess" water begins to flow back to sea very strongly across the lowest point in the sandbar, and this

ONE OF THE THINGS KIDS LOVE TO DO AT THE BEACH IS COLLECT THINGS, PARTICULARLY ROCKS. BEACH ROCKS FEEL GOOD. THEY HAVE BEEN RUBBED SMOOTH BY ALL THAT TUMBLING IN THE WATER. MANY OF THEM ARE QUITE ATTRACTIVE AND INTERESTING JUST AS THEY ARE. BRING SOME HOME TO BE IDENTIFIED LATER OR TO BE PAINTED.

FOR ROCK PAINTING YOU WILL NEED A SET OF ACRYLIC PAINTS (ALREADY MIXED, IN JARS), A PENCIL FOR PRELIMINARY SKETCHING, A SMALL BRUSH FOR EACH CHILD, PAPER TOWELS OR NEWSPAPERS (TO PROTECT FURNITURE), WATER FOR CLEANING THE PAINT BRUSHES, AND THE ROCKS.

HAVE THE KIDS SCRUB THE STONES CLEAN. PAINTING OVER SALT OR SAND DOESN'T WORK WELL. WHILE THE STONES ARE DRYING, ENCOURAGE THE KIDS TO EXPERIMENT WITH A SKETCH OR TWO. WE'RE NOT STRIVING FOR REALISM HERE. A PEAR-SHAPED ROCK CAN BECOME A PENGUIN. A SMOOTH OVAL ROCK CAN BE TURNED INTO A CHESHIRE CAT SIMPLY BY DRAWING A BIG CAT SMILE AND WHISKERS ON IT. THE OLDER KIDS CAN PAINT A PICTURE OF THE BEACH OR THE COTTAGE YOU'RE STAYING IN.

WHEN THE PAINTINGS ARE DRY, PRESERVE THEM WITH A COAT OF WATER-BASED VARNISH. THEY MAKE GREAT PAPERWEIGHTS AND SOUVENIRS. WE HAVE SOME THAT WERE DONE YEARS AGO, AND THEY MEAN MORE TO US NOW THAN THEY DID THE DAY THEY WERE DONE.

When the kids tire of rock painting and sand castles, have them try sand-casting. You'll need five pounds of plaster of Paris, an empty coffee can, a stirring stick, water (can be saltwater), and interesting beach debris.

Have each child dig a "mold" in the sand, a depression that he or she can line with shells or pebbles, make into a face (the nose will go down deeper into the sand), or decorate with patterns using a stick or the plastic forks from lunch. The molds should be dug where the tide won't reach them for an hour. A narrow rim of sand must be built around the edge of the mold to keep the plaster from flowing away. Start with fairly small molds.

When everyone is ready, pour water into the coffee can until you have enough to fill the first mold. Add plaster and stir. Keep adding plaster and stirring until you have thick soup, then stop and immediately pour the mixture gently into the mold. (Saltwater plaster sets even more rapidly than freshwater plaster.)

The mold should be allowed to sit for half an hour, if possible, and then it may be lifted out of the sand very carefully. Just before you leave the beach, brush off any sand that still clings. In a day or so the casting will have dried completely, and it may be painted or scratched to add design detail, or shellacked for permanence.

flow immediately starts to gouge a bigger opening in the bar. Now the water on either side of the opening flows along the bar toward that opening, and then it turns at a right angle and goes out to sea. This is a rip current, the force in an undertow. It can be extremely strong and extremely fast, but it has limitations.

The most important thing to remember is that these currents are usually narrow. Your best course of action is to swim parallel to the shore and cut right across the current. You may find that three or four strong strokes will carry you into calmer water, and you can then proceed to the shore where you will kneel and kiss the sand and vow never, ever to go into the ocean again.

A genuine rip current dissipates rapidly when it reaches deeper water. If you have to go out with it, you will find yourself free of it before too long, and then you can begin working your way back in, farther along the shore. Do just enough paddling to stay afloat and let the normal action of the breakers carry you in. Remind yourself that this current is a limited condition. It does *not* exist all along the shore. Try not to panic.

Before you even go into the water, there are a couple of things you can do to avoid trouble. If there is a big storm out at sea—even hundreds of miles away, in the case of a hurricane—don't go in over your waist because the sea will be feeling the effects of that storm all up and down the coast. Just figure this could be trouble and stay in shallow water. Even on a day when there's no storm out there, spend a minute sizing up the situation before you go in or let the kids go in. You can spot a rip current from the shore because the water looks choppy there and big waves do not usually break on the outgoing current. They break when they hit the shallow bar, but by then the channel opened up by the rip is not shallow. (Even if you are in a small boat, it's a good idea to stay away from choppy-looking water.) Last but not least, the topography of some beaches seems to set people up for trouble more often than is normal. If you hear the same beach named over and over in reports of near drownings, season after season, pick another beach; the lay of the land there is not right for small swimmers.

There is another hazard that gets very little publicity but probably kills more people than undertows do. People just love to climb out on rugged rock formations and watch the surf crash below them. You see it all the time: Dad and two little kids posing for Mom and her camera on the far edge of a rock already dripping with salt spray. Rocks visited by the sea twice daily are usually coated with marine plants or tiny animals that make footing treacherous. Sometimes there will be a wave, or several waves in a row that are a great deal larger than the rest—"rogue" waves. A rogue wave's extra size may not be apparent until it rears up as it enters shallow water, which could be too late. When you combine slippery footing with tons of fast-moving water and the element of surprise, you have instant tragedy. There isn't any mystical name for it. Being pulled off rocks by waves is what it is, and that's what it's called. It doesn't happen every day, but it happens too many days.

Planet Shine—A Soft and Lovely Light

*O*nce in a while when you're stargazing, you will find a big, beautiful star right in the middle of a constellation that is not supposed to have a star there. Chances are you're looking at a planet. There is no point in hunting for planets on your star charts. Planets come and planets go in a predictable, orderly fashion but not on a schedule that coincides with the procession of the stars. You'll have to consult a planetary timetable if you want to identify the brightness in question. Most star guides have a timetable in the back.

Someone may ask, "What's the difference between stars and planets?" Well, there are lots of differences, depending on which star and which planet you're discussing, but the basic difference is that stars make their own light. They burn. Our sun is a star. Planets shine by reflected light, our sun's reflected light.

Demonstrate the difference by lighting a candle in a darkened room. The candle makes its own light, like the stars. Hold a mirror up so the candle's light bounces off the mirror onto a wall. The light in the mirror and the light on the wall are reflected light. To some people, stars seem to twinkle and burn while planets give off a serene, steady light. Do you see a difference?

Our sun has nine planets, and we inhabit one of them. Every planet is different, and as far as we know, the others do not support life.

Only five of the others may be seen in our skies without special equipment: Mercury, Saturn, Jupiter, Mars, and Venus. Mercury hardly counts because it is so close to the sun that it is unlikely you'll see it very often. But there are times when Venus and Mars are the brightest, most beautiful things in our sky.

Planets move along a path called the ecliptic. If you check your star chart, you will probably see a dotted line indicating this planetary highway. Ten to one your unexpected star is on this path. If it is not, you're on your own. A satellite? A U.F.O.?

July

Thunderstorms and Tonsil Lightning

*T*hunderstorms can occur almost anywhere in the continental United States, but their frequency varies greatly. The Florida peninsula averages about 130 storms a year. Some areas of the country have only 2 or 3. At any given moment there are probably 1,800 storms in progress around the globe, and lightning is peppering the planet at the rate of one hundred hits per second. It is thought that thunderstorms return most of the earth's negative charge, which is constantly leaking out into the atmosphere. If this is true, thunderstorms are necessary and beneficial.

Your regular cloud-thumping storm usually begins with a mass of moist, warm air that has been heated by radiation from the sun-heated earth or by passage over warm water. (The convergence of opposing winds can set a thunderstorm off, too.) The heated air separates into cells and rises, expanding as it goes up through the centers of those cells. The higher it soars, the farther it gets from its source of heat, and the colder the air around it becomes. When this moist, warm air cools to condensation level, the dew point, water vapor begins to condense out of it in small droplets. The condensation process itself releases more heat, which fuels the updraft with fresh energy.

Updrafts can lift tremendous quantities of water high into the sky. At the upper edges of their lift, the moist air they carry spreads out from the center of the cell. Eventually it falls earthward again, creating a powerful downdraft. Now the cycle is complete—warm, moist air rising through the center of the system, and cooler, wet air falling on the outer edges of the system. When that cooled, moist air—the downdraft—approaches the earth's surface, it rolls out across the ground as wild, gusty wind, a sudden drop in temperature, and, usually, a short, violent downpour of rain and/or hail. (This downdraft, sometimes called a "downburst," has been held responsible for several plane crashes, and many airports are studying ways to spot downdrafts before they can cause trouble; special equipment can detect them before they are seen or felt.)

Any really tall cloud (and thunderheads are towering) probably tops out over the freezing line in the sky. At temperatures between 32 degrees above and 40 degrees below zero Fahrenheit, water droplets may remain droplets of "supercooled" water, whose temperature is actually well below freezing, until they come in contact with tiny particles called freezing nuclei. Then a droplet becomes an ice crystal and rapidly grows into a snowflake, which eventually falls below the freezing point and turns into a raindrop. So most thunderstorm rain in the mid-latitudes was actually snow or hail for a brief time at a high altitude. Snowflakes that melt into rain and then get kicked back upstairs by an updraft and freeze again, over and over, become hail. When the hail gets heavy enough or falls into the clutches of a downdraft, it comes down to earth. Large hailstones have gone up and down several times, as a rule, and if you examine them, you can sometimes see ringlike signs of layered growth.

The cooling effect of the downdraft reduces the source material for the thunderstorm—heated, moist air—and in a short while the storm will probably put itself out.

Thunderheads are cumulonimbus clouds, tremendous clouds with broad, dark bases, necks rising like castle turrets, and wide-spreading sunlit tops. (When you see that well-known "anvil" top on a thunderhead, it's a sign the cloud cap has gone so high that it's icy.) The base of a thunderhead becomes negatively charged. The top becomes positively charged. (No one is really sure why that happens, as yet, but there are several theories.) At any rate, when the attraction between negative and positive becomes strong enough—*POW!* Lightning may pass between parts of the same cloud, between parts of different clouds, and between cloud and earth. While the earth is usually negatively charged, it becomes positively charged directly under the thunderhead. The earth's negative charge is shoved away by a force called electrostatic repulsion. The cloud's base repels a charge similar to its own in the earth and induces a positive charge. This positive charge on the earth's surface follows the cloud around like a friendly puppy, growing stronger as the negative charge in the cloud above it grows stronger. The positive charge may extend for several miles beyond the center of the storm. Eventually this charge gets so excited, it starts climbing walls, trees, anything that will get it closer to the big negative in the sky.

Air is a very poor conductor of electricity, but at some point the strength of the electrical fields involved (up to one million volts per meter) becomes overpowering, and a stroke called the "pilot leader" heads for the ground, followed a fraction of a fraction of a second later by a current called the "step leader," which advances toward the ground in a jerky, hesitant, branched pattern. When the step leader is close to the earth, a "discharge streamer" from the ground or from something in contact with the ground rises to meet the step leader. Now there is a completed path from cloud (negative) to earth (positive). At this point we get "return stroke," "dart leaders," "secondary returns," and so on, which keep going until all the opposing charges have been spent or the violent movement of the air breaks it all up—and that's the short version of what lightning is.

A lightning stroke causes a mass movement of electrons to strike the air along its path. The heat this generates can reach 18,000 degrees. Those heated air particles expand and move out in a hurry, and a lot of loud compression results—and that's the short version of what causes thunder.

Since the lightning path forked and spread out on its way to earth, compression occurred in a branched pattern. Sound travels 767 miles per hour, much more slowly than light, so the sounds of compression, having varying distances to travel, will reach our ears as a "roll" of thunder some time after we have seen the flash of the lightning that caused it.

The difference in the speed with which sound and light travel enables us to gauge how far away the lightning is. Count the seconds between the lightning flash and the onset of the thunder and divide that figure by five. The answer will be the number of miles between you and the lightning. If fifteen minutes go by without your hearing any thunder at all, the

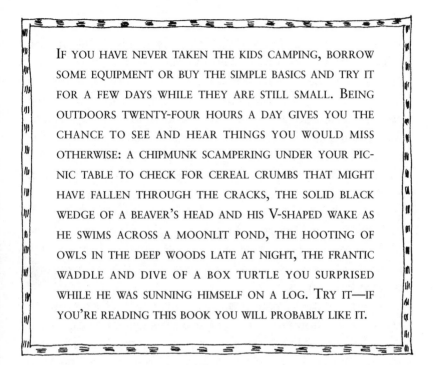

IF YOU HAVE NEVER TAKEN THE KIDS CAMPING, BORROW SOME EQUIPMENT OR BUY THE SIMPLE BASICS AND TRY IT FOR A FEW DAYS WHILE THEY ARE STILL SMALL. BEING OUTDOORS TWENTY-FOUR HOURS A DAY GIVES YOU THE CHANCE TO SEE AND HEAR THINGS YOU WOULD MISS OTHERWISE: A CHIPMUNK SCAMPERING UNDER YOUR PIC-NIC TABLE TO CHECK FOR CEREAL CRUMBS THAT MIGHT HAVE FALLEN THROUGH THE CRACKS, THE SOLID BLACK WEDGE OF A BEAVER'S HEAD AND HIS V-SHAPED WAKE AS HE SWIMS ACROSS A MOONLIT POND, THE HOOTING OF OWLS IN THE DEEP WOODS LATE AT NIGHT, THE FRANTIC WADDLE AND DIVE OF A BOX TURTLE YOU SURPRISED WHILE HE WAS SUNNING HIMSELF ON A LOG. TRY IT—IF YOU'RE READING THIS BOOK YOU WILL PROBABLY LIKE IT.

next roll should be considered the first in a new storm.

Lightning too far away to be seen as forked light or heard as thunder is frequently called "heat lightning."

If you would like to eavesdrop on thunderstorms farther away, tune in on your AM radio. Those crackles and crashes of static are probably interference from a storm at some distance. If you do this often enough, you can develop a knack for gauging direction, distance, and severity of thunderstorms outside your area.

Lightning may occur in other forms, including ball form. For a while there was some controversy about whether or not ball lightning really existed. It exists. We've seen it. We were experiencing what was, even for our hill, a humdinger of a storm one afternoon when we heard lightning hit nearby. It sounded like a rifle shot. A car was coming up our road, and we saw a large ball of orange-yellow light appear over the top of the car. It was about the size of a salad plate or a little larger. The elderly couple in the front seat were three feet or less beneath it, but they never knew that. They drove tranquilly on past our house. The ball traveled with the car, hovering over it, and then suddenly disappeared. The whole thing was probably over in five or six seconds, although it seemed longer at the time.

To avoid close contact with lightning (it still kills quite a few people every year, but the number is decreasing rapidly because people are learning what to avoid), stay indoors as the storm approaches. Stay away from and avoid using all electrical appliances and metal objects. Avoid open doors and windows, fireplaces, and the telephone. Get out of the water and get out of a small boat. If you're caught outdoors, stay away from the tallest objects in the area—far, far away. For instance, if there's a big tree in the center of an open field, *do not* stand under it for shelter. Put some space between you and that tree—twice its height, if possible. Lie down in a ditch or just stretch flat on the ground. If you're golfing, take off those cleated shoes. If you're working with flammable material, stop. And here I must add one of our own rules based on the experience of two people we know of who were severely injured by lightning: Don't go to the john and don't wash anything—your hands, your hair, even the dishes—while a storm is overhead. Just don't.

This next rule is my favorite. If you feel electrically charged all of a sudden, if your hair stands on end and your skin feels tingly, you may be about to be hit by lightning. Experts advise you to drop to the ground immediately. If I thought I was about to be struck by lightning, I would not need an expert to tell me to fall down. I would pass out. The trick would be to get me to stand up again. Ever.

Now that we've covered lightning on a big scale, let's have some fun with tonsil lightning. It begins with the purchase of a couple of rolls of wintergreen Life Savers. Take one of the kids, and a hand mirror, and some Life Savers into a dark closet. Shut the door and let your eyes adjust to the darkness for a few minutes. Then put some of those Life Savers in your mouths and *crunch* with your mouths slightly open. Yes, that is a form of lightning. Blue-green lightning. (If your teeth are getting too fragile for this kind of thing, it's okay to cheat and bring a pair of pliers into the closet with you and crunch down with them. Not as dramatic, maybe, but better than a trip to the dentist.)

For a while the kids are going to be more interested in replicating the experiment and demonstrating it to their friends than in understanding it. But when the jaws tire or you run out of Life Savers, someone may ask how that works.

Sugar in a crystalline form is being smashed and shattered by the act of chewing. As the crystals break, electrically charged crystal fragments—some negative, some positive—are being separated. Eventually (in tiny fractions of seconds) the negatively charged electrons become so strongly attracted to the positive electrons that they cross the intervening spaces, and as they do, they fetch up against the nitrogen molecules always present in the air. These molecules absorb the electron's energy and then release it as a bluish light. Normally this light is not visible to us, because we do not see ultraviolet light, but wintergreen accepts ultraviolet light. When it gets all charged up by these unexpected developments, it releases it as the tonsil lightning you're looking at in that closet. Is that cool or what?

Rainbows on the Grass

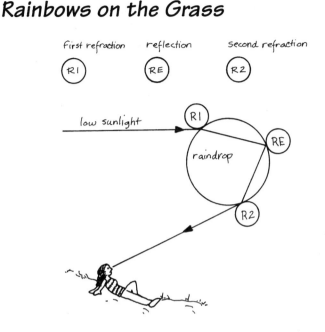

First refraction   *reflection*   *second refraction*

(R1)   (RE)   (R2)

low sunlight

R1

raindrop

RE

R2

Late some afternoon when it's 90 degrees in the shade and the air is thick and blue with humidity, get out the garden hose, tell the kids to get into their bathing suits, and make rainbows on the lawn. (It might be a good idea for you to strip down to a T-shirt and cutoffs as well.)

Crank up the water pressure and turn the hose nozzle until it is almost closed and a very fine spray is coming out, the kind of spray that would blow away if you so much as coughed. Face away from the sun and describe an arc in the air in front of you with that misty spray. You should see a rainbow in the mist. If you swish the nozzle quickly from way down low on your left, up, over, and down low on your right, you can make an almost complete rainbow circle. The arc on the left will still be hovering in the air while the bow on the right is appearing. If you stand on the line between shadow and sunlight so that you can look at part of the rainbow against shadows, that part of the bow will be even clearer and brighter. Very dramatic!

Now let the kids try it. Rainbows, rainbows, everywhere. This must mean that the pot of gold lies somewhere under your lawn, right?

I can see a whole lot of splashing, shouting, and squirting going on here, and it's not likely that anyone will stop in the middle of pouring water into his sister's ear and say, "By the way, Dad, how do rainbows happen?" But when everyone has cooled off and has had time to reflect, someone may ask. And in line with our policy of never leaving a parent unprepared, here goes.

A rainbow happens when a lot of individual drops of water act like prisms. A prism breaks light into its component colors. When sunlight enters each drop, it is refracted (which means, among other things, that its direction is changed) and reflected, and comes back to us separated into color bands and at a great deviation from its original path. Three things must be present for you to see a rainbow: There must be sunlight, preferably at a low angle—late or early in the day. There must be drops of water in the sky or mist over the lawn. You must be standing between the light and the drops of water.

Everyone's rainbow is his or her own unique experience. Your daughter, standing two feet to your right, sees her own rainbow—and it will be infinitesimally different from yours. There is no one big rainbow in the sky that looks the same to everyone on earth.

You may see two "wild" or natural rainbows at the same time. The primary bow, on the inside, will be brighter. The colors will go from red at the outer edge to purple on the inside. The secondary bow will be a reversal of that color scheme— red on the inside, purple on the outer edge.

You can never walk under the bow of a wild rainbow or reach the place where it should touch down. Rainbows will always be off there in the distance or, on very hot afternoons, hovering just over the lawn.

Showers of Stars

*S*hooting stars." The name has an aura of mystery and excitement about it, doesn't it? Even old hands at star watching react when they spot their first shooting star of the evening.

Actually, shooting stars are not stars at all. Scientifically speaking, they are little bits of matter called meteoroids, which range in size from a grain of sand to a bit of gravel, and their trails. Some scientists believe these bits of matter originally came from comets, old, disintegrating comets. When meteoroids enter our atmosphere, they burn up—most of the time. Their trails are made up of hot particles and glowing gasses. These trails may linger for a fraction of a second or, in rare case, minutes. When a meteoroid appears in our sky as a shooting star, it is scientifically referred to as a meteor.

You may have noticed that I said "most of the time" they burn up. Once in a while meteors make it all the way down to the earth's surface. When they do, what is left is referred to as a meteorite.

No need to worry about being flattened some day by a meteorite. You are more likely to die as a result of being trampled by a hairy camel at noon on Fifth Avenue.

Unfortunately, the best meteor viewing usually comes after midnight, which is way past the lemonade crowd's bedtime. Perhaps you would consider getting them up one night after midnight when a very active shower, such as the Perseid shower, coincides with a weekend or a school vacation.

There are significant showers on or about the following dates:

DATES	CONSTELLATION	LOCATION
JANUARY 1–4	HERDSMAN	LOW IN THE EAST
APRIL 19–24	LYRE	HALFWAY UP THE EASTERN SKY
MAY 1–6	WATER CARRIER	VERY LOW IN THE EAST
JULY 26–31*	WATER CARRIER	SOUTHERN SKY
AUGUST 10–14**	PERSEUS	EASTERN SKY
OCTOBER 18–23	ORION	HALFWAY UP THE SOUTHEAST SKY
NOVEMBER 14–18	LION	LOW IN THE EAST
DECEMBER 10–13	GEMINI	OVERHEAD

*Peak should be July 28.
**A major shower. Probably one of your best bets. Peaks on August 12.

You might see a meteor on any clear, dark night of the year, from twilight on, but if you really want to see a lot of them in a relatively short time, plan to spend a pleasant hour or so outdoors during a regularly scheduled shower. It will take your eyes up to thirty minutes to adjust to the darkness. During a good shower, you could, if you were lucky, see as many as fifty meteors in an hour of peak activity, but most of us are happy if we see one every couple of minutes. Don't strain to watch every inch of the sky every minute. Just look up and relax. If there is a bright movement up there, your eyes will catch it and follow.

When we give you the constellation of origin, we are just giving you a place to start watching. Meteors can streak across the sky from almost any angle, so it's a good idea to sort of scan the sky casually every few minutes.

The kids will really enjoy this once they're awake. Being up so late is exciting in itself. Lying outside rolled up in quilts, sipping hot cocoa and nibbling on apples while overhead the shooting stars flash by—that's living. But check the sky *before* you wake them in case this particular shower is proving to be a disappointment (that happens sometimes) or a cloud cover has moved in. You don't want to be stuck with a gaggle of wide-awake, excited kids at 12:30 at night and nothing to do with them but turn on the television.

The Care and Feeding of the Red Eft

*I*f you will be walking in the deep woods sometime this summer (and if not, why not?), watch for red efts. These efts, also known as red-spotted newts or salamanders, are really not red. They are more of a soft coral-orange color. They're quite small, perhaps 1½ to 3 inches long, and they move rather slowly. Their little feet scramble along when they're alarmed, but not much progress results. They are very easily caught.

In the hand they are incredibly light, and their skin is delicate, almost dry to the touch, and smooth. Two lines of jew-

eled dots run down their backs. They look as if Fabergé had designed them for someone's velvet lapel.

A red eft is an amphibian. It hatches from an egg laid in a pond and spends its first summer in the water breathing through gills. Then it develops lungs and crawls out onto the land, where it spends the next three or four years. Finally, to complete the life cycle, it returns to the water where it undergoes a color change, grows a finned tail, and reproduces.

Besides breathing through its lungs, the red eft is capable of respiration through its skin when it's moist and through the lining of its mouth. It is vital, therefore, that the kids handle it gently and that they never leave the eft in a situation where it might dry out. You find red efts near moist situations—fallen trees that retain lots of rainwater in their rotting wood, mossy banks and lakesides, and damp leaf litter.

There are few amphibians with the charm of the red eft. If the kids would like to bring several home for their terrarium, it can easily be arranged. We've kept them over the winter many times. (We release them back into the woods each spring.) When the windchill factor is below zero and the view out the window is of a landscape frozen as hard as bone, it's refreshing to look into the terrarium and see moss and ferns glowing green under the lamplight, the wintergreen sporting its bright red berries, and a pink salamander reclining under a tiny pine tree.

At times all the efts in our terrarium would disappear—hibernating—but then they would show up again when the spirit moved them. It is important to keep the terrarium suitably moist even when the efts are hibernating. They will still be respiring through their damp little skins. Remember where you found them and try to duplicate that same dewy, cool atmosphere.

Scoop up some silver-dollar-size pieces of moss and a little soil for your efts to travel on, and then work those into the terrarium when you get home. Moisten the moss they'll be traveling with before you leave the woods.

Efts can pretty well feed themselves in an open, natural terrarium. We would put tiny bits of ripe banana or apple on the moss to attract small insects for them, and we dug up very small earthworms for them every so often. If an eft is getting enough to eat, it looks plump and smooth. When it is not, its little sides begin to cave in and its skin wrinkles. You can tell that it needs a good square meal.

We had a small eft colony in our terrarium one year, and as winter came on and the ground grew cold, we were forced to use bigger worms than usual because of the number of efts we had to feed. The efts seemed undaunted. But one day as we laid the sacrificial earthworm on the moss and one of the efts seized it, the worm turned. Actually, it reared up and tossed that eft over its shoulder, if a worm could be said to have a shoulder. The eft hung on—either it was even more afraid to let go or it had been caught off guard and needed time to think. The worm, flushed with success, tossed the eft back down onto the moss in front of it.

We stood there aghast, afraid that if we interfered, we might do more harm than good. We could hardly believe what we were watching. The worm was not nearly as big as the eft, but apparently it was muscular. Eventually, after a spirited tussle, the eft either let go or was shaken loose. We scooped up the worm and replaced it with a tiny bit of ground beef, waggled in front of the eft on the end of a broomstraw. (Food has to be moving to really appeal to efts.) The eft was too upset to eat right then, but it recovered completely later.

We realized that we would have to serve these larger worms cut up (ugh!) into small eft-size pieces, lay in a supply of ground beef and broomstraws, or set up a worm farm to produce a steady supply of very small worms. We did all three. (I don't know why it distressed us to cut up a worm when all of us had, at one time or another, put worms on hooks and gone fishing with them. We know that worms are such primitive little creatures that their ability to feel pain is nonexistent or very, very slight. But it seemed different somehow, and we could hardly bear to do it, even with our eyes closed.) The ground beef on straws was very time-consuming and never all that popular with the efts, either. In the end we settled for worm farming to keep a supply of tiny worms coming. We lined a sturdy cardboard box with newspapers, tossed in a handful of wet leaves, a handful of potato peelings, and a trowelful of dirt from the garden. More papers, leaves, peelings, and dirt. We finished off with a light layer of papers. We put a dozen adult worms under the top layer, moistened it all down, and turned off the light. The worms spent the winter happily in the box doing what worms do, and there were lots of tiny worms eventually.

There is no need to worry about worms leaving their home spread. They don't ramp around. You won't run into one of them out on the kitchen floor one night when all you wanted was a glass of milk to help you sleep. In the spring you'll have plenty of them to go fishing with or to release into the garden where they can industriously till and fertilize the soil.

● ☆ ✳ ○ ◎ ◉ ○ magnitude
5   4   3   2   1

A Swan by Starlight

*F*rom June to November there is a Swan circling through our night skies. She is gorgeous.

The Swan is a big constellation. The image you should try to pick out is that of a large bird flying down the Milky Way headed south. The bird will be just to the east of the zenith (the invisible point right over your head). Her wings will be out-stretched. Her short legs will trail behind her, away to the northeast. Her long neck will extend down the center of the Milky Way.

The Swan's body and head are outlined in lovely, bright stars, but the best of them all will be Deneb—a sort of taillight for the Swan.

August

Rock Hounds and Their Quarry

*T*here's gold in them thar hills. . . ." Also agates, diamonds, amethysts, tourmalines, quartz crystals, and aquamarines. All over this country, in almost every state, amateurs are still finding precious and semiprecious stones.

Few things stir a child's imagination (or acquisitiveness) like a real treasure hunt. Panning for gold and rock hounding are fascinating projects for family vacations and weekend trips. Someone in the family may actually find a valuable stone, but even if nothing extraordinary shows up, you'll probably come home with a few handsome, collectible specimens.

If the kids are at all interested—and that's like saying "If the sun continues to rise in the east"—borrow a guidebook from your local library or buy one. Insist on a volume that has color pictures, and explicit, detailed information on where each mineral is to be found. Passing through the visitor's center on the Maine Turnpike once, I picked up *Gems and Minerals: A Guide to Rockhounding in Maine* by Jane C. Perham. This was just a little book, but it had a description and a color photograph of forty-four different minerals found in Maine and information such as, "Fuschite is found only in the Wolf Neck area of Freeport" and "Columbite occurs in Albany at the Pingree Ledge and the Wentworth Mine." This is the kind of information you need. By the way, among the forty-four minerals listed in Maine (and Maine is not generally thought of as being a "mining state" like Colorado or Nevada) are gold, amethyst, smoky quartz, rose quartz, citrine, aquamarine, tourmaline, watermelon tourmaline, garnet, topaz, and freshwater pearls (not a mineral formation but eagerly sought by collectors anyhow).

A great many old mines are still open and operating for the tourist trade. Many of the old quarries are open to the public for gem hunting now, too. In most cases where the hunting is done on privately owned and maintained property, a small fee for hunting is charged, and in some cases if a valuable gem is found, the operator is entitled to a percentage of its worth. If you can't find a good rock hound's guidebook, write your state department of recreation or your tourism board, or contact the geology school in the nearest state university.

This is a hobby that everyone can get into. The littlest ones, being built close to the ground and having youthful 20/20 vision, seem designed by nature for exactly this kind of search. The only problem is that at that age they love everything. They are world-class appreciaters. They will find a thrilling specimen about every five minutes and go home so loaded down with pebbles that they can hardly walk. Well,

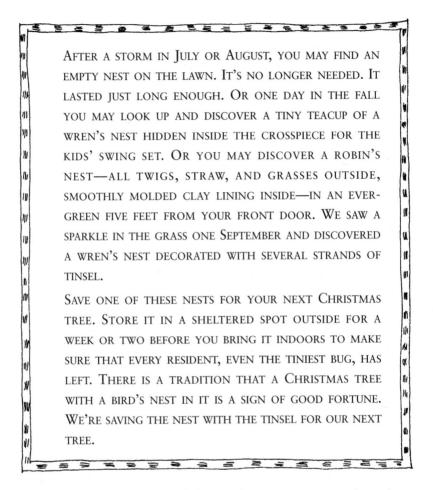

AFTER A STORM IN JULY OR AUGUST, YOU MAY FIND AN EMPTY NEST ON THE LAWN. IT'S NO LONGER NEEDED. IT LASTED JUST LONG ENOUGH. OR ONE DAY IN THE FALL YOU MAY LOOK UP AND DISCOVER A TINY TEACUP OF A WREN'S NEST HIDDEN INSIDE THE CROSSPIECE FOR THE KIDS' SWING SET. OR YOU MAY DISCOVER A ROBIN'S NEST—ALL TWIGS, STRAW, AND GRASSES OUTSIDE, SMOOTHLY MOLDED CLAY LINING INSIDE—IN AN EVERGREEN FIVE FEET FROM YOUR FRONT DOOR. WE SAW A SPARKLE IN THE GRASS ONE SEPTEMBER AND DISCOVERED A WREN'S NEST DECORATED WITH SEVERAL STRANDS OF TINSEL.

SAVE ONE OF THESE NESTS FOR YOUR NEXT CHRISTMAS TREE. STORE IT IN A SHELTERED SPOT OUTSIDE FOR A WEEK OR TWO BEFORE YOU BRING IT INDOORS TO MAKE SURE THAT EVERY RESIDENT, EVEN THE TINIEST BUG, HAS LEFT. THERE IS A TRADITION THAT A CHRISTMAS TREE WITH A BIRD'S NEST IN IT IS A SIGN OF GOOD FORTUNE. WE'RE SAVING THE NEST WITH THE TINSEL FOR OUR NEXT TREE.

they had a good time, and that's what you were out there for, right? As long as you don't have to weigh them and pay by the pound as they leave . . . .

Older children can really get into this. Someone may eventually branch out into gem tumbling and polishing (kits are available for the hobbyist), and someone else may be so pleased with the results that he or she will be inspired to try jewelry design. The serious-minded may become interested in geology, and the holy terror may decide to spend his or her time searching for arrowheads. And there is always that thousand-to-one chance that you might find something that is really, really valuable.

When the Moon Hits Your Eye . . .

*H*ave you ever thought that when the full moon was overhead, it didn't seem nearly as large as it did when it first rose? And did you wonder if you were just imagining it? Common sense tells you that the moon does not deflate as it climbs higher in the sky or reinflate as it descends at dawn. Still, it looked about three times bigger coming up over the horizon than it did at midnight, to you.

Well, almost everyone gets that impression, and there is even a term for it now: the moon illusion. Lots of interesting explanations have been put forth over the centuries. The most interesting fact of all is that so far none of these theories fully and satisfactorily explains the illusion. For instance, some think that when we see the moon rising behind far-off trees or buildings, our minds do a little rapid arithmetic and jump to the conclusion that since the moon is coming up behind one, two, three, four big pine trees, it must be humongous. Then, when we see the same moon high in the sky with no pine trees around, we wonder why it looks so much smaller. If that was all there was to it, though, how do we explain the fact that people watching the moon rise over the sea or desert—both flat-line horizons— still see it as a big, gorgeous globe, and see the midnight moon as much smaller?

To prove to yourself and the kids that it is an illusion, ask one of the children to take a picture of the moon as it rises and another when it's overhead. Measure the moon in the developed pictures. Or extend your arm full length and cover the moon overhead with the tip of your little finger or an aspirin, or a bead—whatever will just barely conceal it. Tomorrow night as the moon rises in all its magnificence, see if that same aspirin or bead will cover it completely at arm's length. It will.

So what's your theory?

What We Did This Summer

Summer is winding down now. School looms. Already the days are noticeably shorter. It might be nice, some rainy afternoon, to create a collage, a small, three-dimensional sampler of what this summer was like, and a record of the first steps in some new directions for members of the family. Did someone start a shell collection while you were all at the beach, or photograph wildflowers up close, or begin learning about butterflies or beetles or songbirds' egg shells? Representative specimens of almost any new collection can be fitted into the collage. In fact, they will make it all the more interesting. And most kids will have duplicate items, spares, that they might agree to display. The only specimens I can think of that would require extra care are rocks, but if the collector is willing to tumble some small stones until they are light enough to stay glued to an upright surface, that should solve the problem. If tumbling is out, perhaps the rock hound could take a heavy hammer, an old towel, and a couple of big, not irreplaceable specimens out to the driveway, wrap each

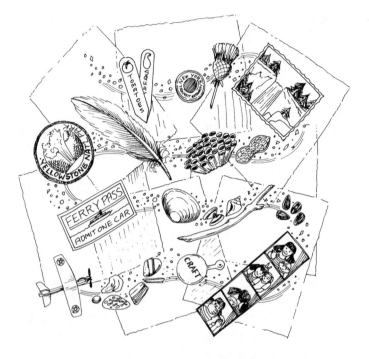

specimen in the towel, and give it a good whack with the hammer (adult supervision is suggested), which should result in lots of small specimens. These can be painted with a clear finish (everywhere but where the glue will be applied, on the flattest surfaces) to highlight their natural color and show off their grain.

Gather all your small summer souvenirs—family snapshots, ticket stubs, campground passes, maps used on summer trips, brochures, choice bits of driftwood, bird feathers—and lay them out on the table. Check the pockets of shorts and duffle bag linings, and look under the seats in the car. Then group the collector's materials separately and see what possibilities suggest themselves.

Before you take any more concrete steps, you will need a backing for the collage, something fairly stiff. The best collage we ever made started with a big traveling-circus poster we took down from a telephone pole after the circus had come and gone. This poster was all bright reds and yellows. It was pretty gaudy, actually. You can use a poster, a canvas board from an art store, a piece of thin plywood, or, least expensive of all but just as serviceable, the bottom of a sturdy cardboard carton.

To tie the various elements of the collage together visually, lay sheets of colored tissue paper over your backing and slap some ordinary white glue, thinned with a little water, on it with a big brush. The tissue paper can be all one color in various depths— one thickness here, three thicknesses there—or different colors. Don't worry if it wrinkles while wet or even tears a little. It won't matter later. Just proceed with joyous abandon and let the tissue rip or bunch up where it may.

It will take a while for the tissue to dry, which will give you time to decide how to lay out the collage. Some groupings practically arrange themselves: Steven's butterflies hovering over a fan of Stefanie's wildflower pictures; Robin's seashells clustering around that bit of silvery driftwood you liked so much. The souvenirs can be placed to flow around or frame the collections, or to form a pattern of their own, weaving down the poster like a trail followed by the family through the summer. The first night out on your trip to Nashville you stopped at that little church for a ham 'n' bean supper, and here's one of the supper tickets from someone's pocket. Maybe that could go in the upper left-hand corner. Halfway to your destination, at a program on dinosaurs, Janet took a picture of Beth with that handsome ranger. That picture could go here, superimposed on a piece of the map of the dinosaur park. Down near the bottom of the poster would be a good place for the pass they put under the windshield wiper on that ferry. There were so many people waiting to go across that they just jammed the cars in on the deck, and Dad was sure we were going to sink because there was actually water coming over the front of the ferry all the time it was crossing that river.

Some children are less interested in making a family collage than they are in making a statement about their own individual effort, such as "Look at these rocks! I got some great samples. And it wasn't easy." Well, if it took considerable time and energy to amass a collection, that effort deserves respect. The collage could serve as a frame for samples from everyone's collections, and these collections could be labeled or identified by a summer snapshot of the collector in the middle of each grouping. Paint a big tree on your backing and place the snapshots and collections on the branches as if they were apples or blossoms (a "family tree" if we ever saw one).

Once you have all agreed on a general plan, set the souvenirs and collectibles on the dried tissue backing to see how they look before you start gluing. Experiment. Move them around. Everyone should feel free to express an opinion because this is one of those projects where there is no right or wrong way to do it, just your family's way.

When you do glue the collage material down (use Elmer's glue), work from the center toward the outer edges so items that stick up won't get bumped or catch on someone's sleeve. And several people can work at the same time that way without getting in one another's way.

It's amazing what you can glue to a collage. We found that even a small balsa wood airplane—the type that is rubber-band powered—would stick. The air was full of small airplanes that summer, looping the loop, soaring from the upper windows into the trees on the other side of the lawn, spinning earthward in a determinedly suicidal rush. We were all pleasantly surprised when our one surviving plane settled onto the collage as if it were making a three-point landing, and stayed stuck. No problem.

Let the finished collage set, lying on a level surface, for a day or two before you hang it. If something falls off, try again or replace it. And even after a summer collage has been hung, additions can be made—a bit of dried seaweed from the Labor Day clambake, the headlines about a late-August hurricane, a few seeds from the last watermelon of the season.

Years from now, or even during the short, dreary days of the coming winter, you will find yourself standing there, gazing at the collage, remembering. And all the memories will be in sharper, more detailed focus because these small mementos were part of the scene at the time. You can run your fingers along the big white-and-brown duck's feather and see the reeds and the lake clearly. You can touch the rough, cheap paper of the ferry pass and feel cold river water coming in through the toes of your sneakers.

Now that, right there, is what we did on our summer vacation!

Tempest in a Coffee Cup

*C*onvection is a process whereby something warm under something cool rises while the cooler, heavier substance is pulled down by gravity. Convection keeps coming into the conversation whenever we discuss weather, particularly turbulent weather, as in hurricanes, thunderstorms, wind, and rain. It even plays a part in renewing the planet. Remember the subduction process associated with tectonic earthquakes? One plate—a slab of cooled minerals, really—slips under an opposing plate and slides down into the fiery core of the earth, and then, sooner or later, it resurfaces as lava erupting in a trench under the sea or boiling up out of the throat of a volcano, making new earth.

If you would like to watch convection at work right under your nose, pour yourself a cup of hot black coffee and pull your chair up to a strong light. Look at the surface of the coffee from a side angle—with the light hitting at an angle, too—do not look straight down on it. Do you see a pale pattern of swirls and squares on top of your coffee? Each light-colored patch is bordered with a thin black line. The whole surface is in constant, gentle motion. The effect is very much like looking into a kaleidoscope.

The light-colored patches are created by individual molecules of water that evaporate from the surface of the hot coffee and coalesce into small droplets as they rise to a point just above the surface. The droplets hang there in an uneasy balance between the downward pull of gravity and the upward thrust of more evaporating molecules. They are little cloud patches, really, and because they are separated from the dark coffee and reflect light, they appear cloud-white. The dark lines are the areas where cooled coffee is sinking back into the hotter coffee below. Every few seconds or so one of the black boundaries will go shooting across the surface, breaking into and dividing the clouds. The heated air right over the coffee has an effect on the cooler water droplets, and then almost immediately dissipates.

Watch your coffee cup. You will find it absolutely hypnotic, and the kids will find that it makes convection real, and easy to grasp, figuratively and literally, instead of something that occurs under the earth or high over their heads, measured in thousands of feet or miles of rock.

A River of Birds Overhead

When we think about migration, the first word that comes to mind is usually "birds." Other species may migrate, but we are most aware of and made restless by the departure of our summer birds. For something that takes place predictably twice every year— something that a great many people have observed, recorded, and talked to one another about—it's amazing that bird migration is still largely a mystery. There are theories about how birds know when to leave and where to go—everything from the earth's magnetic field, the angle of sunlight, the orientation of the stars and moon, to a sort of species' memory of a proven route—but none of the theories has so far been proven to account for all migratory behavior. In the end it will probably come down to a combination of signals or just a mystery.

There is a vast network of unmarked trails that drains this country of migratory birds from north to south as if it were a watershed. These trails are called "flyways" which is a beautiful and appropriate-sounding word. There are generally considered to be four major flyways on this continent. If you could see them laid out on a map of the hemisphere, they would look like continent-size trees. The branches and twigs reach up into Canada and the northern tier of states. The trunks follow geographic landmarks like coastlines, river basins, fertile plains, and mountain ridges. The roots spread out into the warm soil of Florida and the other southern states, Mexico, Central America, and, in a few cases, South America.

If you live under a flyway, you will see the birds flowing over your head during the day and hear them beating steadily to the south at night, but only if you remember to look up and listen. If you live near a flyway, you may see flocks of birds headed east or west, soon to be drawn into the mainstream and turn south with their companions. It is said that there is no area of the United States that doesn't witness some migration overhead. So get ready!

Across the country, migration usually begins in August. There is a day—it falls so often on August 28 that we have come to expect it then—when swallows swirl up over our meadow and pool in a dizzying aerial whirlpool for several hours and then leave. At ten in the morning, particularly if it's a lowering, cloudy day, the air over the yard will be constantly stirred by rising and falling spirals of birds—hundreds of birds. Our place must draw them from all over town, perhaps because we're on a hill and they are preparing to catch the prevailing winds. They twitter to one another while they fly, and their calling also rises and falls. If you are alone in the house and not particularly fond of birds, it can begin to prey on your nerves, like a scene from Alfred Hitchcock's movie. You find yourself looking out the window every few minutes. There is an eerie, restless, uneasy feeling abroad, even in the house. Perhaps the same atmospheric changes that urge the swallows to leave have an effect on humans, too. Then, on one of your quick checks out the window, you see a blank sky. You look again. There are no birds out there. None. Every swallow is gone, and even the birds you would normally see, of different species, have not yet returned to their normal activities in the area.

The tide of migration continues to flow south until Thanksgiving or even later. Every time you step outside, take a moment to look up. At first it may seem you're looking up a lot on the odd chance that something is going on up there, but after you have spotted your first few V's of geese, your first great flock of birds flying so high you cannot even identify them, you'll be hooked. You'll start to look up without even thinking about it and develop a sixth sense for those times and places when conditions are right and something is going on up there. It pays to listen, too. If you hear a sound someone once described (perfectly) as the yelping of a pack of small dogs, look some more because that means Canada geese are going by.

Check your feeders when migration is going on, because you will see visiting birds you may not see at other times of the year or for another couple of years. Look for "erratics"—birds found far from their regular breeding grounds or migratory routes who have been blown off-course by high winds or a storm. To learn what else is going on in yards around town, look in the white pages of the telephone book to see if your area has an Audubon hot line. Maybe the bird lover in the family could call the hot line once a week and report back to the family. Maybe, if he or she gets serious about this, that person could become a contributer to the hot line, too.

Even at night, when you step out of the car, listen. Small birds migrate at night, and they seem to call to one another constantly. We don't know exactly why they travel in the dark, but it may be because darkness provides protection from predators and because they need to rest and feed in the daytime. I was sitting at a picnic table around two or three in the morning one September night. The table was poised at the edge of a rocky point overlooking Casco Bay in Maine. The weather was overcast and the cloud cover was very low. Suddenly I became aware of a twittering overhead, a rush of wings, a crescendo of small bird calls. I heard but could not see thousands of little birds flying by, heading out across the bay. I felt as if I might touch wing if I stood up and stretched out my arm. In a few minutes they were gone and the last twittering had faded away. It was a memorable moment. So listen, even when it's dark.

In the pursuit of any interest, whether it's drag racing or stamp collecting, there's usually one premiere event, one moment you know is not likely to come again. My bird-watching moment happened when we were living in Virginia. Our home was in the foothills of the Blue Ridge Mountain. The house overlooked a broad valley and a far range of mountains. I was standing in the living room one afternoon, looking out the front window, when I noticed scores of birds flying overhead, a ribbon of birds floating out across the valley toward the distant mountains. They were flying very high. I have no idea how long they had been passing over before I looked up. The distance swallowed them long before they reached the far horizon. Halfway across the valley they became just grains of pepper against the clouds, then a blurred wisp of smoke and then, no matter how I strained, invisible.

They never stopped. The ribbon flowed on and on. Sometimes it narrowed to one or two birds flying hard to catch up with the group ahead of them (and I found myself urging them on, worrying about them); sometimes the ribbon broadened until it was twenty or fifty birds across and many hundreds long.

The sun went down, and I tried to find a way to ease my neck and legs. I had been standing still with my head back for so long, I was in real pain. Still they came on, and I could not turn away from that window. I had never seen anything like it—a river of birds. When I absolutely, positively could no longer distinguish bird from cloud, I drew the drapes. But I knew they were still going past, flying over our house and out across the valley to whatever lay beyond the mountains.

I hope I have convinced you. I hope that for the next three months you're going to look up and you're going to listen. I hope you'll remember to watch the feeder and check the Audubon hot line. And I hope that one day you will see a river of birds overhead.

The Big Serpent Holder in the Sky

The first time I saw the Serpent Holder, I didn't know I was looking for him. We were stargazing at Acadia National Park, and the ranger said, "Look for a big old campfire-style coffeepot about halfway up the southern sky." I had no trouble finding that coffeepot, and neither will you. If you're facing south, the handle will be on the western side of south, the spout on the eastern side of south, and it is a *big* coffeepot.

Once we had all located that pot, the ranger told us we were actually looking at the Serpent Holder. The serpent is in two pieces—trouble in paradise, apparently. The snake's front end is flailing around fairly high in the southwestern sky; its head is a small circle of stars. Its tail is the spout on our coffeepot and several smaller stars just over the spout. The Serpent Holder's feet are shuffling along just below the bottom of our pot.

The Serpent Holder, Ophiuchus, is thought by many to represent a god of medicine in Greek mythology, Asklepios, who

may be linked to a real Egyptian physician, Imhotep, who lived almost three thousand years before Christ. You can hardly scrape the surface of astronomy without learning something about the old civilizations. The stars have always been important to man, and he was seeing things in them and trying to understand their order thousands of years ago. Maybe one of the older children could look up the Greek myth about Asklepios and Hades, the god of the dead, and Zeus and Orion. It's an interesting story. Most of the tales in mythology are full of action, high emotion, and harrowing consequences. It explains why Orion, the Serpent Holder, and the Scorpion (a constellation at the Serpent Holder's feet) are never allowed to appear together in the sky.

With all due respect to our Egyptian physician, however, begin by finding that big campfire-style coffeepot in the southern sky.

September

Hurricane Warning

Some people cherish the illusion that hurricanes are just bigger than average storms. When you think of them that way, you get that warm little glow of confidence that so often precedes catastrophe. Hurricanes are a class of weather all by themselves. The more you learn about them, the greater the respect you have for them.

A hurricane usually begins life over a wide area of sun-heated ocean water. The water probably has to be at least 80 degrees, which is why hurricanes are classified as tropical storms. As the heated air rises, a small low-pressure area is formed. This begins to involve and influence winds flowing over the warm sea. The winds come into this low-pressure area, turn, and rise. All this warm, moisture-laden air ascends until it begins to cool, at which point the water vapor in it condenses into clouds. Condensation releases more heat, which keeps everything warmed up and headed up and out. The earth's rotation puts spin on this rising column of heated air (counterclockwise in the Northern Hemisphere), and the whole process begins to intensify and speed up. More and more warm air is pulled into the low-pressure area, where it rises and, under the influence of the earth's rotation, spins. A huge whirling cloud chimney of warm, moist air is forming.

Bands of rain begin to feed into the chimney, and it is now a potential hurricane. The rainfall under these bands can be heavy. The bands show up on radar very clearly and are considered a distinctive indication of a new hurricane.

No one knows why some areas of warm, moist air and disturbed winds combine to form a weather system but not a hurricane. No one knows what decides which tropical disturbances will grow into monster storms and which ones will merely sigh and dissipate. There is still a lot about hurricanes that we don't know.

If a real hurricane is forming, the system intensifies and spreads out and starts to travel. When a hurricane is young, it moves fairly slowly, perhaps ten miles an hour. It may pause and hover in one spot while it gathers strength. When it begins to move again, watch out! It may travel at twenty to thirty miles an hour or a great deal faster. It may proceed in a gentle arc, recurving out to sea, or it may loop the loop, or it may strike directly inland. We know that hurricanes frequently travel from east to west and then recurve from the southwest to the northeast. Sometimes land appears to deflect their forward motion, and high- or low-pressure areas may cause them to alter course. Meteorologists can only keep us posted on what a storm is doing right now and project possibilities and probabilities. With hurricanes, you never know.

Soon the eye inside the chimney walls of fantastically powerful winds becomes more clearly defined. It may be almost cloudless. From above, the hurricane resembles a ragged doughnut. The eye and the chimney are a pumping system, providing and delivering the energy for the hurricane.

We cannot stop hurricanes or dissipate them. Perhaps we should not try. Anything with that much force (it is not unusual for an Atlantic Ocean hurricane to be as powerful as 500,000 Nagasaki atomic bombs) could be a relatively harmless way of restoring or maintaining some vital atmospheric balance. If there were no hurricanes, the alternatives might be worse.

We have learned enough about hurricanes to provide adequate warning when they are approaching land. This should mean that while we can only protect our property to a certain extent, no lives are lost to hurricanes anymore. It should mean that, but it doesn't. Some of us still look on hurricanes as spectator events. It is important to remember that hurricane winds can be as high as 150 to 200 miles an hour. Winds like that can shove a freight train off its track. And since hurricanes come to us from the sea, waves are a problem. Not just big waves, giant waves. And along with these mountains of water comes the surge—the force of water that has been shoved toward us by high winds, across hundreds of miles of open water, day after day. The lower barometric pressure accompanying a hurricane actually causes the ocean to bulge under it, which adds to the surge. In Rhode Island

Sound in 1938, the hurricane surge was seventeen feet. When I try to imagine giant waves coming in on top of a surge like that, my hands begin to perspire and my feet shuffle restlessly—sort of like running in place, if you get my drift.

In addition to the wind, wave, and surge activity, we have the rain. Hurricane rain, under those rain bands, is more like a body of water settling on the earth. It is practically wall to wall H2O. Many places get six to twelve inches in a fairly short period of time. The flooding, earth slides, and dam failures resulting from torrential rain are perils some people forget about until the water starts rising over the doorsill. If you live in an area that sometimes floods under normal storm conditions, move to higher ground.

One of the most treacherous features of a hurricane is the "eye," that calm, sometimes sunny center of the storm. The most intense, violent winds of the whole storm are usually right around the eye. It sometimes happens that when the eye passes over a storm-lashed area, the weary inhabitants, thankful for their apparent escape, go outdoors to inspect the damage—and never make it back. The other side of the eye slams into the area with no warning and catches them still outdoors. The winds are coming from the opposite direction, now, and a great deal of additional damage may occur since everything in the hurricane's path has already been stressed severely and the ground is saturated with rainfall.

As the hurricane approaches, your radio and televison stations will warn you to get to a safe location before it strikes. This is very good advice.

A small group of us were trapped by a hurricane once on a low-lying sandy peninsula that stuck out into the water from a long cape. We had been warned to evacuate, so we packed up and headed for the mainland, but the wind got so strong so quickly that the state police had to close the bridges going off the cape. (Cars were being pushed into the side rails and vans and trucks were being overturned at the high points on both bridges.)

We went back to the cottage. The five o'clock weather advisory said the worst of the storm would soon be over. But the clouds did not break and the wind did not die down, and around eight o'clock the local meteorologist broke the news on the radio that the hurricane had turned again unexpectedly and was coming across the cape. We decided to drive into town, park on the street, and sleep in the car. At least we would be on high ground. I went out to start the car.

When I turned my flashlight on the dirt road behind the cottage—the only road off the peninsula, I felt sick. Literally. While we had been keeping an eye on the storm as it pounded the beach in front of the house, it had been creeping up on us from behind. The road was completely under water. The rising tide and storm surge had combined to force the inlet on the other side of the road to overflow its banks. This happened in less than an hour. There were no posts or trees to tell me where the shoulder and the drop-off into the inlet were. The water could be eighteen inches or four feet deep at the low points down the road. We could still try the road before the water got any deeper or the night any darker, but if I misjudged and we went off the road into the inlet, we would have to climb out of a partially submerged car and walk a mile through the hurricane and rising water.

We could stay put and ride out the storm in a three-room summer cottage huddled behind some low dunes, but if the sea came over those dunes, there would be nothing to stop it from carrying the cottage right into the inlet behind us. And we had a little girl with us. We put our only life preserver on the child and settled down in the cottage. Every few minutes someone would get up and shine a flashlight through the front window to see if the water was starting to come down the path between the dunes. We had decided that if the waves broke through from the front, we would abandon the cottage, link arms, and try to walk out just above water level on the road, going from the protection of one dune to the next, hanging on to each other no matter what. It was a long night.

Finally, in the small hours of the morning, a watery glow showed through the racing clouds: The moon was breaking through. The wind began to abate. The storm was passing.

After breakfast we went out to inspect the damage. The waves had come very close to broaching the dunes. Another foot or two of high water, and we would have been afloat. The beach was as smooth as a sheet of brown paper, under a collection of driftwood, lobster pots, Styrofoam floats, ropes, timbers from docks, and several dead gulls. The car, parked behind the cottage in a little hollow, was draped and flecked with green—shredded seaweed that had become airborne.

If I were doing it again, I'd dump everything in the car and go as soon as we were asked to evacuate. If I were turned away at the bridges, I'd find high land in town and spend the night there in the car or locate a shelter. If you evacuate promptly and the storm turns and your area escapes undamaged, don't feel sheepish. You did the right thing.

In honor of its being the hurricane season, the kids might like to decorate their own version of the Beaufort scale, a scale developed by scientists to gauge and compare wind speeds by the effect they have on our surroundings. The finished product can be mounted on the fridge. Each child can pick a wind speed category and draw something appropriate—charming or terrifying as he or she sees fit. Then if a

THE BEAUFORT WIND SCALE

MILES PER HOUR	RESULTS
Under 1	Smoke rises straight up
1–3	Smoke drifts, wind vane (except for the one for chipmunks, see March) does not respond
4–7	Leaves rustle, wind vane responds, can be felt on skin
8–12	Leaves and twigs are stirring, light flags blowing, street debris in motion
13–18	Street debris and dust blowing, small branches tossing
19–24	Small trees and large branches swaying
25–31	Big branches tossing and wind whistling in wires around house; umbrellas turning inside out
32–38	Whole trees swaying; walking into the wind is hard
39–46	Twigs snapping off; walking into the wind is very slow
47–54	Roofs may be damaged, with shingles and slates blowing off; branches breaking
55–63	Isolated trees uprooted or snapped off
64–73	Widespread damage to trees, signs, chimneys, antennae
Over 73	Damage and destruction severe

storm should strike, any kind of storm, you can tell how many miles per hour the wind is blowing by comparing the effects with your own personal Beaufort scale.

Bulbs for the Forcing

September is the time to shop for bulbs for indoor winter bloom. Right now our inclination is to focus on the outdoors as much as possible—the weather out there is so pleasant. But it takes time to prepare a bulb for indoor blooming, about five minutes right up front and then eight weeks of benevolent neglect.

The most dependable, satisfying, and inexpensive bulbs for forcing, if this is to be a child's project, are the Paperwhite narcissus. Paperwhites are determined to bloom, and nothing short of being cooked will stop them. Their flowers are lovely to look at—white, delicate, and lustrous. Their fragrance is so rich that in a small room it can become almost too sweet.

Buy a handful of bulbs for each child. Pick bulbs that are plump, solid-feeling, and cool to the touch. Round up some gravel or pebbles at home or buy plain white gravel. If you can't find it in the garden shop, try the pet store. Ask for aquarium gravel.

You will need a bowl or pot for each clutch of bulbs, something several inches deep. It must not have a drainage hole. If it is transparent so the kids can see the bulb roots developing, so much the better. We usually end up buying inexpensive bowls because the way we go through bowls around here, we can't afford to tie any of them up for almost three months. If you have some charcoal briquettes left over from the summer

cookouts, it's a nice little touch to let one of the kids pound a briquette to smithereens and drop a few pieces in the bottom of each bowl. Charcoal helps keep the water fresh and sweet. Pounding helps release latent hostility.

Now you should have bulbs, pebbles or gravel, charcoal, and bowls.

Drop a few bits of charcoal into the bowl, fill it almost to the top with pebbles, and wiggle the bulbs, fat side down, into the pebbles until they are pretty stable. Add water until it comes just below the base of each bulb. Place the bowls in a fairly cool, dark spot and leave them alone for six to eight weeks. The only attention they will require is watering once in a while, when the water level recedes too far from the roots and bulb bases. Maybe each child could be responsible for checking on them during a certain period of time (and, unknown to all, you might also check every week or two).

If the bowls are transparent, as the weeks go by you should see strong white roots stretching down through the gravel and water to the bottom of the bowl. There may be some pale green growth starting at the tops of the bulbs. Since we want a really good root system below each bulb before we permit it to bloom, we keep them in their cool, dark environment until the bowl is full of roots. The bulbs may actually be pushed up to the top of the gravel as the root systems grow. That's fine. No problem.

When the eight weeks are over or the root systems are well developed, bring the bulbs into warmth and light gradually, giving them a couple of days to get accustomed to each stage.

Once the flowers open, they will last a lot longer if they are not placed in direct, hot sun for very long. Keep them cool and give them plenty of light. They will perfume the whole room.

If you start them in late September, they will provide a lovely counterpoint to all the red and green ho-ho-ho! of the holiday season. If the kids are willing, you might pot up one set of bulbs in late September, another during the second week of October, and a third just before Halloween. Date each pot to keep them straight. This succession planting will keep the house smelling like spring for a month or more.

You might ask the school-age kids to figure out how it is possible for bulbs to grow and bloom on just pebbles and water. (The answer is that everything the plant requires to bloom, except for moisture, is already packed inside the bulb.)

September

Monarch Butterflies—A Royal Mystery

Another migration takes place under the bird-filled skies of autumn. Chances are it has eddied and flowed around you, actually brushed up against you, and you never noticed. The monarch butterflies go south every fall. They are the big, gorgeous orange-and-black butterflies that haunt milkweed patches. Their migration poses as many questions as the bird migrations do, and maybe more.

For years it was known that several million monarchs from the western states went to a place called Pacific Grove in southern California every fall. They clung to a group of Monterey pines all winter, leaving their trees only once in a while for brief periods of time. It was not known where the monarchs from the eastern states went in the winter.

Then in 1975 a colony of several million monarchs was discovered in Sierra Madre, Mexico, by Kenneth Brugger. He contacted Dr. Urquhart, who, with hundreds and hundreds of volunteers had tagged thousands of monarchs over the years. (Can you imagine attaching a tag to the wing of a butterfly without damaging it? Egad!) Together the following winter, in January 1976, they found one butterfly in that Mexican colony with a Minnesota tag. When you think of the work involved and the part that chance must have played, finding a tagged butterfly in a crowd like that was a small miracle. Since then it has been recorded that eastern monarchs winter in small areas of Florida, the Yucatan Peninsula, and the Guatemalan Peninsula, as well as the highlands of Mexico. Western monarchs winter at tiny refuges from Mendocino, California, to Baja, Mexico. Some of the butterfly refuges have recently been lost to development—which is hard to understand or believe; the monarch's migration is now considered an "endangered phenomenon."

There are many mysteries that cloud our view of migration, but one of the most intriguing concerns the monarchs of Pacific Grove and Sierra Madre (they sure have an affinity for places with romantic, exotic names). These butterflies die after they start the cycle again by laying eggs in the spring. The eggs are laid on milkweed at points on the route going north or right after the butterflies reach the northern limits of their range. As of this writing, no one is sure that any monarchs get all the way home again, or if any do, how many, but tagging work is going on constantly, and sooner or later we will find the answer.

The eggs may hatch in about two weeks, but by that time, most of the overwintering parents are dead. The newly hatched larvae spend several weeks as caterpillars and then go into a chrysalis for two weeks. When they emerge as butterflies, they resume the trek north, if that is necessary. Once they've reached the northern states, they live out their life cycle, lay eggs, and die. Their eggs hatch and repeat the cycle. The last generation—the butterflies that hatch in late summer—eat just like their predecessors ate but metabolize differently. They actually manage to acquire a little stored body fat, no doubt in preparation for their journey. One thing is sure: The monarchs we see heading south in September and October are at least several generations removed from those who started the same journey the year before.

How do they know when to leave and where to go? What instinct prompts them to dare deserts and long flights over rough water? How do they find the same traditional trees on a Mexican mountain at nine thousand feet when all they or their parents have ever known are Vermont meadows or

Illinois gardens? How is that knowledge transmitted? It would be a feat similar to you and I starting out for the Amazon River with very few provisions, no maps, and no prior knowledge of exactly where the Amazon was. Even turning south, if you lived in the United States, would be a decision you would not be properly prepared to make. So how do they do it? Everyone has a theory, but no one really knows. Put the kids to work on this some rainy weekend. Years hence one of them may actually come up with the answer.

And why should we care? Well, some people care to learn just because they don't know, like climbing a mountain because it's there, but there may be more practical benefits to be gained. Some important clues to the genetic transmission of information or instinct may be revealed when we study the monarchs. And it's possible and perhaps even probable that the monarchs are responding to signals and clues that we ourselves might someday utilize if we could just learn to receive and understand them. Is there anything we do now as navigators that even approaches what this fragile, short-lived little insect does by the millions every year? I don't think so.

It is possible to order kits containing "butterfly boxes" and chrysalises from places such as Papillon Park, 120 Tyngsboro Road, Westford, MA 01886. If you are traveling near one of the butterfly gardens or atriums in this country (Butterfly World, Coconut Creek, FL; Butterfly World, Vallejo, CA; Cecil Day Butterfly Center, Pine Mountain, GA; Papillon Park, Westford, MA), it would be well worth your time to stop and visit. A unique experience. And even the smallest toddler will enjoy it.

I bought myself a butterfly box the other day. It contained two small clear plastic cups with lids. Each one held a spoonful of what looked like green paste and a spiky little caterpillar clinging to the side of the cup. These caterpillars, the instructions said, would turn into painted lady butterflies if I just left them alone long enough. Everything each caterpillar needed was contained in its small plastic cell.

The caterpillars spent most of their time eating, nibbling at the green paste, and resting. After two days one of them began attaching himself to the lid of his cell and hanging upside down to form a J for several hours at a time. The other caterpillar became so quiet, he appeared to have died. Fortunately I couldn't bring myself to give up on him and heave him out. Not yet.

On the third day the J-hanging caterpillar tried it one last time and stayed put. Twelve hours later he looked very strange, as if a glaze was seeping out from the pores of his body to cover him. Twenty-four hours later the glaze had formed a knobby shell around him. Only his most prominent spikes were still visible, sticking out beyond the chrysalis. The chrysalis then turned a dull golden color. It hung there for eight days. There was no sign that life still existed within it.

The day after the first caterpillar hung up his spikes, the second one came to life again, ate voraciously for a few hours, and followed his example—followed it in every detail, down to the timing by the hours.

On the eighth day, as I walked past the chrysalises, my heart did a double beat. One of them had gone dark. I put my glasses on and bent down. No. Not dark as in dead—dark brown with orange spots. I was watching butterfly wings take shape inside the chrysalis. The next morning I saw that the first butterfly had come out. The transparent shell was split open, and below it on the shelf was a painted lady pumping up its wings, tremulously getting used to space and air and sunlight again.

I had set up a butterfly corner with flowers these butterflies were known to prefer, homemade butterfly nectar, lots of sunshine, and high ceilings—everything a butterfly could desire. Except freedom. After watching my painted lady fly to the windows and bang softly into them again and again, I carried him or her on a notebook to the door, opened it, and held the butterfly up to the sun. It took off instantly—zooming away, riding the breeze higher and higher until it cleared some tall pines across the yard and disappeared.

The second butterfly was so quiet, so trembly, I felt it would not survive the rigors of outdoor life. After all, this was September, and the nights were getting cool, the winds were picking up, and flowers were getting scarcer every day. But the message was unmistakable. Time and time again it, too, went to the windows and waited. So I took it to the door and released it, figuring a life of thirty minutes doing what it wanted to do was preferable to a life of a week or so as a prisoner. To my astonishment it acted exactly as the first had, pumping its wings vigorously and rising over the pines as if it was born to fly, for heaven's sake.

Prisms in the Window, Rainbows on the Wall

As we move into fall, more and more sunlight finds its way into our houses. Instead of riding high in the sky, the sun is low and farther south, and its rays angle in through our windows. This is the time to start looking for the old lead crystal prisms that used to hang from antique lamps and chandeliers, at the harvest festival jumble tables in your town, or at yard sales. You can sometimes pick up prisms for fifty cents each. They are frequently piled together in an old shoebox, off to one side. Before you buy one, rub it on your sleeve and then take it to a sunny window and hold it up. Does it reflect a rainbow onto the walls or floor? If not, pass it up. There is quite a spread in the quality of old prisms. You want the ones that throw some color around.

The kids may already have heard, of course, that all the colors of the rainbow are present in sunlight. What's harder to grasp is how the prism sorts them out so we see a rainbow on our wall. All the colors in light move at slightly different speeds and travel through different materials at different speeds. For instance, glass or water will slow them down. The colors also differ in the degree to which they refract, or bend, going through glass or water. Purple will bend the most, red the least. Once you know this, you will notice that red and purple are always on opposite sides of the spectrum. Their rates of speed and their refraction behavior separate them forever.

Wash each prism in a mild mixture of ammonia and warm water. Polish it dry and tie it on a length of nylon fishing line, which is practically invisible against the light. (Heat the knots over a candle or match flame until a little melting together takes place—an adult job, of course—which will make the knot permanent.) Then hang the prisms in a sunny window. Hang three or four of them in a cluster or a row, on lines of different length. Everyone who enters the room when the sun is coming through that window will feel more cheerful. Guaranteed.

You can buy brand-new lead crystals at New Age shops or nature stores, but the old ones are better for our purposes.

Their glitter is softer and their colors more subtle, and they're a lot cheaper. They make delightful child-to-relative gifts. We packaged ours in rainbow wrapping paper and wrote on each label, "This box contains a rainbow. Handle carefully and open in a sunny window." They were received with genuine delight, I think. When the recipient is an elderly relative, you might want to assume the responsiblity for getting the prisms hung in an appropriate window.

Dawn in the North—Aurora Borealis

The aurora borealis—northern lights—is really spectacular. If you've never seen it, make a point of glancing up once or twice when you first go out at night, because you never know when it might flash on. They can take many forms—arcs, rays, spots, or just a glow. Some are transparent white, others are softly colored, and an occasional display is brilliantly stained. They appear to originate in the north but may fill the sky over your head. If they are not brightly colored, you might assume that you're seeing a very odd cloud formation. If you can see stars clearly through the "cloud" and the cloud is moving rapidly or in a strange manner, and seems to be fanning out from the north, chances are you're looking at northern lights. Watch a little longer; you never know what might come next.

The first time I saw them, I had been out stargazing for some time. My eyes had grown accustomed to the dark. Suddenly I became aware of a shifting, swaying veil of white light in the north. While I stood there wondering, the veil swung out across the sky. The movement was so sudden, so unexpected, and so overwhelming—like a skywide white curtain blowing in the wind—that I yelped and jumped back.

If you live near the 40th latitude, you might see the lights ten or twelve times in the average year. The farther north you go from there, the greater the frequency of sightings. (Unfortunately, the farther south you go, until you pass the equator and start approaching the south pole, the less frequent the sightings.) If there is an unusual weather or astronomical occurrence going on, our local meteorologists call it to everyone's attention on the evening news. This is a big help, and we would miss a lot without it. Ask your local station if their weather person could do the same for your area and remind you about eclipses, comets, solar flare activity, and meteor showers expected.

Naturally the kids are going to want to know what causes the northern lights. Well, the current theory is that they are the result of electronic bombardment of the earth's ionosphere, the part of our atmosphere about sixty miles up. And where do all these bombarding electrons originate? The answer seems to be in solar flares, sun spots. When there is a great deal of solar flare activity, scientists have come to expect an aurora borealis display within two or three days. The flare emits tremendous quantities of electrons. They shoot through space until they hit our ionosphere. A disturbance results, and, it is thought, the electrons follow the earth's magnetic field toward the poles. That is why there are northern lights and southern lights—aurora australis.

Aurora is a Latin word meaning "the dawn," and *borealis* is also a Latin word meaning "north." Therefore, aurora borealis means "dawn in the north." That's quite appropriate. Aurora australis means "dawn in the south." The name of the display you will see depends on which hemisphere you live in.

There are years with above-average sun spot activity, and this seems to go in predictable cycles. So if you hear that especially vigorous solar flares are expected, remind everyone to look up. Good show!

The Autumnal Equinox and a Model for the Seasons

*S*eptember is the month in which we celebrate (if that is the right word) the autumnal equinox. Actually, there is more than a hint of melancholy around this equinox. We are entering the period of short days and long nights, and winter is waiting in the wings.

To mark the occasion we will create the Simplest Possible Symbolic Representation of the Celestial Seasonal Samba. We will illustrate how the earth is tilted a little to one side as it rotates and how that condition causes us to have seasons. We are going to do this without taking out a loan on the house for equipment or devoting a week of evenings. When we say "the Simplest Possible . . ." we mean it.

You will need one orange, one rubber band or ponytail holder, one clove or thumbtack, one match, one knitting needle, long pencil or skewer, and one candle.

Run the knitting needle through the center of the orange, starting at the end where the stem was attached to the tree. The needle should stick out an inch or so beyond the orange at both ends. Slip the rubber band around the orange the other way, so it girdles the orange at its waist, its widest part. Consider the knitting needle an axis around which your orange will spin. Think of the rubber band as the earth's equator. Somewhere about halfway between the top of the orange and the equator, stick your clove into the rind. It will represent Cleveland or Boston or Baltimore—wherever you live.

It is time to turn the lamps down low and light our candle, which will stand for the sun.

Ask one of the kids to start turning the orange around and around slowly. When the side with the clove in it is facing the candle, Baltimore is having its day. When that side is facing away from the candle, it's nighttime in the city.

While the orange is turning—night/day, night/day—have the child start walking around the candle. Now the earth (our orange) is circling the sun (our candle). Finally, have the child tilt the orange a little—23 degrees, actually (that's about one-fourth of the way down from the perpendicular to the horizontal or from standing up to lying down).

Now we have our earth (1) revolving on its axis, (2) spinning gracefully around the sun, and (3) tilted slightly to one side like a small top that is losing momentum. Sometimes light from the candle hits our clove (Baltimore) a glancing blow, but when the orange is on the other side of the candle, the clove faces the candle straight on and candlelight falls more strongly upon it. Winter occurs when the sun's rays hit us at a wide or oblique angle. Summer occurs when light from the sun strikes us more directly.

By the time everyone has had a turn spinning and orbiting, the facts of the case will be firmly implanted in every little mind. Time to blow out the candle and say good-bye to summer and hello to fall.

October

A Thousand Years in a Nutshell

If ever there was a month made for afternoon walks, October is it. The air is cool and brisk, the colors are spectacular, and you can see for miles. Get on out there and take all those hikes you planned to take this year, before the days get any shorter.

On your way home organize an acorn search. If you live in the eastern two-thirds of the country, you should have no trouble finding acorns. The trick is to find acorns of the type you would most like to plant in your yard. The prize should go to the person who finds an acorn under a white oak *(Quercus alba)*. Why, you may ask. I was coming to that.

Many of the really ancient oaks you hear about are white oaks. The Charter Oak, a white oak that grew in Hartford, Connecticut, was estimated by experts to be between eight hundred and one thousand years old when it died. (The heart of the tree had been damaged by then, so a completely accurate count of the rings was no longer possible.) When you plant a tree like that, you're reaching for immortality. What was going on a thousand years ago? (Can the kids come up with something?) Well, William the Conqueror was taking England by storm in 1066—remember reading about the Norman Conquest? And the first crusade started off for Jerusalem in 1095. Saint Francis of Assisi was born in 1182. Who was living where you live now, a thousand years ago? The continent wasn't what you'd call crowded then, but one of the primitive Native American peoples was probably at least passing through your area every year.

Odds that your particular white oak will live a thousand years are pretty small, given the hazards of our present environment, but isn't it nice to hold something in the palm of your hand that at least has that potential?

White oak acorns are noticeably sweeter than most acorns and, for that reason, scarcer. Squirrels go for them like kids for penny candy. If you want to find some, better get out there and hunt for them soon. Look for the tree first. The biggest branches of the white oak are at right angles to the trunk. The bark is light gray on the younger branches, deepening to dark gray on the more mature wood, and the buds on the bare branches are rounded and fairly small. When you rub the bark, some scales may come off on your hand. White oak leaves have rounded lobes and stay on the tree, looking pale, a long, long time.

The whole shape of the tree is massive—very masculine and

solid-looking. You get the impression that this tree means to stay a while, pardner. The acorns are not on stalks but are attached directly to the small branches. They are about ¾ inch long. The little cap on top is sort of warty-looking and covers about one-fourth of the acorn.

If you do not find your white oak acorns soon after they fall, give it up until next year. They freeze and die if they haven't sprouted and put down roots by the time really cold weather comes. Fortunately, the white oak, which is also a very desirable tree commercially, is present from southern Maine to northern Florida and from southeastern Minnesota to eastern Texas, so the chances are good that you live within hiking distance of at least one.

Cultivate the soil for your acorn. Dig deep, turn the dirt over and break it up, and add a little dried cow manure. Then plant the acorn just below the surface of the soil, or plant several. You can always thin out the weaker plants in the spring and give them away. (Be mindful of the fact that oaks put down deep roots; and take up your extra oak seedlings with as little disturbance and as much soil as possible.) Finally, protect your acorn. A circle of chicken wire (preferably spray-painted white before installation) will keep dogs, softball players, and the kid who mows the lawn from killing it inadvertently when it sprouts. Water it deeply to get it well started, then go indoors for a cup of something warm.

There is a line in Sir Walter Scott's *The Heart of Midlothian* that seems appropriate right now: "Jock, when ye hae naething else to do, ye may be ay sticking in a tree; it will be growing, Jock, when ye're sleeping."

Do you ever wonder who will be living where you live a thousand years from now? It could be a race very much like the one living there right now but taller, perhaps, and more peaceful—or another group of Native Americans starting over. Either way, the squirrels will still appreciate those sweeter acorns from your white oak. And in the perfect marriage of the romantic past and a hopeful future, keep your eye out for oak saplings cloned from the Major Oak, the tree most closely associated with Robin Hood in Sherwood Forest, in folklore. Yes! An outfit named Micropropagation Services is actually cloning the Major Oak and hopes, some day soon, to offer these little chips off the old block for sale. You heard it here first!

The Autumn Leaves . . .

*T*o say that the leaves change color in the fall in the cooler states is like saying that Mae West finally got over being shy. All summer the trees modestly formed a cool green backdrop while roses, rainbows, and butterflies softly strutted their stuff. Sometime in September the trees began to shoulder everything else aside and took center stage. Now there are days when their color is so vivid and there is so much of it, we experience sensory overload. Yellows shimmer in the sunlight as if they were lighted from inside; oranges and reds flare like torches along the roads; wines and shades of chartreuse warm the old stone walls. All this glory is hard to ignore, and no one should ignore it. So if the kids fail to ask how the trees change color, bring it up.

The yellow pigments have been there all the time in the leaf. They are covered by a layer of green—chlorophyll—throughout the spring and summer. (If someone asks how the yellow layer got there in the first place, you're on your own. My policy has always been that the best defense is a good offense. Ask the child to look that up.) Fall weather conditions and changes in the sunlight retard the formation of chlorophyll. The green layer of cells sort of bleaches out, and there it is—a yellow leaf.

The reds are produced by anthocyanins—red pigments carried in solution in the sap. Sugar in the sap aids in the production of anthocyanins. When the temperature gets down to 45 degrees or lower (but not so low that real frost damage occurs, which would put an end to vivid coloring), sugar is not removed as rapidly from the leaf, so the sugar and the anthocyanins build up and—presto!—a red leaf or leaves tinted with red.

A leaf carrying anthocyanins will be reddest where it receives the most sun. Cool nights and sunny days favor the production and accumulation of this pigment—and our brightest fall foliage displays.

A certain type of child will trot right out after a discussion of fall coloring and find himself a green leaf, and tear it in half looking for that layer of yellow. Then he will shred a red leaf and run the pieces over his tongue, tasting for sugar. Keep your eye on that kid. He may not have totally accepted your explanation of how the leaves turn, but he is probably going to be the one who supports you in your old age with the money he gets from his patents.

Three Cheers for the Owl

*F*eather for feather, pound for pound, few birds do us as much good in a concrete, nonsymbolic way as owls. We hardly ever see them and rarely hear them, but they're out there, and would we ever miss them if they disappeared. Have you heard any calling in your neighborhood at night lately?

We hear our resident owls a lot more often in the fall. This might be partly because the nights have gotten quieter as the weather has gotten colder (the ranks of the insect chorus diminish with each chilly evening) or because we are suckers for atmosphere, and in October, the Halloween month, owls are definitely in, or because many owls "call" more in the fall and early winter to let other owls know where their territorial boundaries are. Territorial rights may be disregarded or taken more lightly in late summer when owl fledglings have left the nest and their parents are ready for some R and R, but the reestablishment of territory must precede courtship, which, in the case of owls, frequently occurs in wintertime. Whatever the reason, listen up when you go out in the early evening.

If you don't know whether you have any owls around, ask yourself if you have any hawks. An expert birder told me once to consider hawks and owls as two sides of the same coin—one hunting in the daytime, the other at night. The relationship doesn't stop with that. Apparently owls frequently use old hawk nests instead of building their own, which means there must be substantial territorial overlap.

When an ornithologist describes owls as our most useful bird, he is referring to the owl's appetite for rodents. A specialist in owls, the late Lewis Walker kept track of what one pair of barn owls brought home to feed their young over a period of ninety-six days. The total was 758 rodents and one bird. If you have ever tried to get rid of a family of mice or rats in your basement, you will have some respect, possibly even affection, for a pair of birds who could round up 758 of them to feed their fledglings.

By the way, barn owls do not insist on living in a barn these days. The two Mr. Walker monitored were living in a church belfry in the middle of Flushing, New York.

If someone asks you how come scientists know all about what owls eat, the answer lies in the fact that owls are not dainty eaters. They tend to bolt their food, and there are some parts of lizards, rats and snakes that even the most cast-iron stomach cannot handle. So hours after dinner, when you'd think he would have forgotten all about it, the owl routinely coughs up small pellets composed of the fur, bones, and so forth, that he has decided to give back. Scientists collect these and analyze them. (I must say it strikes me as not just coincidental that the adjective "dedicated" is so often applied to scientists.)

Owls cannot really rotate their heads all the way around without stopping, as they do in cartoons, nor can they swivel their eyes to either side like most other birds can. Their eyes face front, like ours. But they certainly can swivel their owly little heads 180 degrees (or half a circle) each way, and two halves make a whole. Their distinctive big-eyed appearance is due partly to their large, front-facing eyes and partly to the feather "discs" that surround their eyes and greatly emphasize them.

Most owls fly and hunt at night. The specialized construction of their flight feathers makes their flight silent, which is probably one of the big reasons for their astonishing success as predators. In the dark, the rats can't see them coming, and with their silent flight, they can't hear them coming. It might almost make you feel sorry for the rats.

By the way, if you think you don't need help in rodent control, think again. It is a rare neighborhood that doesn't support a thriving population of rodents. We just don't see them very often, because that is the way they want it. I have seen Brother Rat boldly sashaying out the back door of a well-known restaurant in mid-afternoon. I have seen frisky little groups of rats frolicking on the banks of rivers that flow through big-city parks and are the settings for many a romantic picnic or pop concert. One major U.S. city is currently spending a lot of time and money to determine how best to contain and dispose of the huge displaced mouse and rat population it will face when it puts in a new tunnel and mid-city highway. Maybe they should invest in an owl breeding program.

Many Audubon centers sponsor evening "owl walks" at this time of year. Why not call your nearest chapter and ask if it is planning something along those lines this month? And when you're out walking with the kids, see if you can find some feathers—not necessarily owl feathers, just feathers. Check out the location of the center rib—the quill—on each one. Flight wing feathers will have a rib near the leading edge of the feather. On the downstroke, which is the stroke that lifts the bird in the air, a lot of air pressure hits each flight feather, and the quill or rib stabilizes and strengthens the feather at the point of stress. The closer the feather to the edge of the wing, the closer the rib to the leading edge of the feather. A feather that helps to clothe the body of the bird will be almost symmetrical; that rib will run right down the center of the feather. Maybe the kids can find and identify some of each kind, flight feathers and "coat" feathers.

Does the Woolly Bear Really Know?

*T*here are those who predict the severity of the coming winter by estimating the abundance or scarcity of berries, the thickness of the coats on squirrels or the bushiness of squirrel tails, the skins of apples, or the nut crop. Some people measure bark or decide on the basis of the date of the first snow. But the controversy reaches its height over the innocent head of the woolly bear caterpillar. (This is a teddy bear of a caterpillar—chubby, fuzzy, and honey-colored along most of his one- to two-inch length, with a dark brown cummerbund around its middle.) Does the width of the stripe around his waist in any way foretell how bad the following winter will be? Discussions on this subject can get heated and are carried on from one fall to the next. The only party we haven't heard from is the woolly bear.

Certainly there are great differences in the width of that stripe. Some of those who believe the differences are significant say that the broader the band, the easier the winter. Some hold the opposing point of view.

Ask the kids to locate a handful of woolly bears this month, and measure their stomach bands. Is there any noticeable similarity among them? The woolly bears, I mean. If so, the orderly one in your group might record the results of your family's survey and stash the statistics in a safe place until spring. (Just trying to measure something that curls up the moment you touch it should keep them busy and entertained for hours.)

It is amazing how much determination and instinct can be packed into a small, humble head. Intercept several woolly bears as they start across a neighborhood road and turn them around so they will be facing the other way when they uncurl. Ninety-nine times out of one hundred those caterpillars will swing ponderously around to their original direction and resume their trip. Pick them up, walk down the road a few yards, and set them down in a new spot. They'll still know where they were headed. Roll them around for a second or two with your finger (gently!) or put them down behind a tree; as soon as their little heads clear, they'll take up where they left off, headed in the right direction. At least it's right to them. It isn't a very big head, but it's a very determined head with an admirably clear vision of where it wishes to go. (During all this measuring and turning, it is important to remind everyone that the woolly bear is alive and fragile and deserves to be handled with kindness.)

Sometime around April the family can decide how they would classify the past winter, and make an appropriate notation on the calendar. This is how a lot of science works: careful observation, the recording of facts and results, an interpretation, and then a restaging of the experiment to verify or disprove the initial results. Next October have the kids round up a new group of woolly bears and measure their racing stripes. (Wider? A milder winter? Narrower? Should we sell the house now and get out while there's still time?) By the second April you and everyone else in the family will probably have a strong opinion, confidently held, on woolly bears and winter weather.

Perseus and His Variable Leg

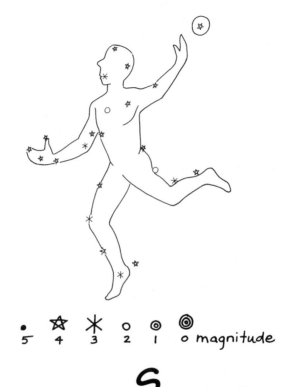

S tarting late this month you should look for Perseus in the eastern sky, a little above the horizon and a little to the north of due east. Perseus will appear to be running down the sky toward the horizon. One arm is flung back up into the Milky Way as if he were saying good-bye. The other is folded back toward his chest. He wears a beautiful second magnitude star at his throat and a variable star, Algol, where his right (from our viewpoint) leg joins his body. This makes him special.

Algol, which is Arabic for "prankster," seems to burn brightly for about two and a half days, dim down for five hours, then burn brightly again. To catch the full effect you'll have to be lucky that first night or go out several nights in a row. The secret behind this variableness is that Algol is a binary star, a double star—two stars revolving around each other. When the darker star is to one side of or behind the brighter star, Algol shines at us in all his glory. When the darker star is passing in front of its twin, for five hours, Algol dims. One out of every five stars, approximately, is a binary. Algol is one of the most famous.

November

Terrariums—Woodlands Under Glass

Kids love building things, and they love miniatures. They can create their own little corner of the woods by building a terrarium, and it will be a learning experience because once a terrarium is established, it becomes a self-sufficient little world unto itself. Its air and water are constantly being recycled by its plants. They renew the air and give off water vapor (by a process called transpiration), which collects as condensation on the glass and runs back down onto the moss, thereby starting the whole process over again.

Begin the project by selecting a clear glass container with an opening wide enough to admit your or your child's hand. Brandy snifters are not your only option. I've seen nice little terrariums planted in mayonnaise jars, fish tanks, beer mugs and candy dishes. It is better, however, to pick the thinnest, clearest glass you can find or afford. Thick glass does distort and blur details. Later on, if you want to get fancy, you can use big containers with tiny openings. (For those you'll also need a special, long-handled tool designed just for terrarium use. You can usually find it in garden stores or florist shops. If not, try using culinary tongs instead.) Avoid patterned glass, which will break up and distort the view into the terrarium.

Place a thick layer of moss, green side out, around the bottom and lower third of the container so the soil will not show through. Then put down a sparse but chunky layer of gravel or shards from broken clay pots and a small handful of charcoal pieces. (One of the kids will enjoy smashing a charcoal briquette in a paper bag with a hammer or a rolling pin.)

Look over your plant material and decide on a plan—high here, low over there—with a little path or a small pond down in front. Encourage everyone to suggest alternatives. Place your tallest plants first, moving them around to see how they look, adding a little soil as necessary to hold them in place. Not too much soil. The container will fill up quickly, and you don't want rampant growth in a very restricted space.

When the major plants are in place, fill in around them with your smaller plants and moss. You can fold and break large sections of moss or cut them with a knife in curving lines. They will merge together and blend beautifully in a very short

WHEN COLLECTING MATERIALS FOR YOUR TERRARIUM, THINK OF THREE LEVELS: GROUND LEVEL—MOSSES AND ATTRACTIVE PEBBLES OR A BIT OF MOSSY WOOD; INTERMEDIATE HEIGHT—SMALL (TWO INCHES OR LESS) PLANTS SUCH AS PARTRIDGEBERRY, WINTERGREEN, OR WHATEVER EVERGREEN PLANTS GROW IN ABUNDANCE IN YOUR AREA AND APPEAL TO YOU; AND TALL—FOUR- TO SIX-INCH-HIGH BABY PINE OR HEMLOCK TREES, OR SIMILAR MATERIAL.

SPOON UP ENOUGH SOIL WITH EACH PLANT SO THAT THE ROOT SYSTEM IS NOT DAMAGED. PLACE YOUR PLANTS IN PLASTIC FOOD STORAGE BAGS UNTIL YOU GET HOME, TO KEEP THEM MOIST. COLLECT MORE MOSS THAN YOU THINK YOU'LL NEED, BECAUSE LINING THE BOTTOM OF THE CONTAINER WILL TAKE PLENTY.

AFTER DIGGING UP A PLANT, PAT THE REMAINING SOIL AND DEAD LEAVES BACK INTO PLACE SO THAT SURROUNDING PLANTS WILL STILL BE PROTECTED. TAKE ONLY PLANTS THAT ARE ABUNDANT IN YOUR WOODS.

time. As the children work, pass around a magnifying or reading glass. It will make working with tiny plants more entertaining for the kids and more interesting for the adults.

A woodland path may be created with tiny rounded stones or cut-up pine needles. A mirror pond can be placed directly on the soil, with moss brought up to cover its edges for a natural look. A real pond, if your terrarium is to be inhabited by amphibians, can be just a small measuring cup—⅓- or ¼-cup size—sunk to moss level. A "log"—really an old twig or bit of bark—would look nice lying beside the path or pond or even going down into the water. If you add miniatures, and children love those little ceramic frogs or rabbits, keep them small. No terrarium will have room for all the things we've discussed. Pick two or three and avoid a cluttered look.

When everyone is satisfied with the design of the terrarium, lightly spray the plants with water. Then go over the glass with a damp sponge and a dry tissue to leave it sparkling clean. Cover the terrarium opening with a piece of clear plastic food wrap or a piece of window glass cut to your specifications at the local hardware store and well sanded around the edges. Some people tie a thin piece of red or green velvet ribbon at the neck of the container, and it does add a dressy touch.

If the cover mists up almost immediately—a heavy mist you can hardly see through—take the top off for several hours and let the terrarium dry out a little. A light, barely visible mist with an occasional drop trickling down is ideal. If no mist forms, add ¼ cup of water. Once you have hit a balance and can see that light mist, the terrarium will thrive and grow without much further help.

If you have amphibians living in your terrarium, you can leave it uncovered all the time and water more often, or, if they are the type that will escape, cover the terrarium with a circle of fine screening that has been pressed into a snug fit or tied in place with a ribbon so the air in the terrarium will not get stale.

Every week or so, check to see if the mist is still forming on the glass. Does the soil feel dry? Are the plants losing their crispness? If they are, add water one tablespoonful at a time over a period of several hours until the proper balance is restored. If any plant gets too large, cut it back with manicure scissors.

Terrariums make ideal gifts for invalids, the elderly, and office workers who need something green for their desks, but can't give it much space or time. They should not be placed in direct sunlight because it will create a buildup of heat that will kill your plants. Light is necessary, but sunshine is not. We did, however, have very good luck this winter with a large terrarium that received just the first hour of sun every morning, so a little sunlight at a low, low angle is not harmful.

It's a small world . . . .

Birds at Your Window

*I*f you are interested in feeding your wild birds—and it an activity that is both fun and educational—decide first whether you're willing to sign on for the duration, until insects are abundant again in your area. Will you be able to keep the feeder stocked? If you go away for the weekend, will you feel free to ask your neighbor to come by and refill it once a day? In bad weather, a bird can starve or die of exposure if he cannot get enough food to stoke his inner furnace. Twenty-four hours of hunger, in extreme weather, can do him in. Once the birds have settled around your place (and a feeder will certainly draw them), food must always be available.

If you are still with me, and I hope you are, here are a few suggestions.

Avoid metal fixtures when possible. Don't hang suet in wire cages. A warm, moist eye might stick to that metal at 10 degrees and be injured. (When you were a kid, did you ever touch something made of metal with your tongue when the temperature was way below freezing? Not more than once, I'll bet.)

Some birds prefer to feed on the ground, others, up. Sprinkle a little seed on the snow around the feeder.

Don't give them lots of straight, undiluted peanut butter. Most of them love it, but it tends to gum up their insides with tragic results. Add cornmeal, oats, seeds, or melted suet—anything birds like that will break up the peanut butter somewhat. Pack this glop into the crevices on a big pine cone or spoon some into half an empty coconut shell and hang it from a branch. (This is the kind of thing little kids love to do. It's messy, but no one cares. You can't make a mistake, and it's in a good cause—a combination that doesn't come along too often in a child's life.)

We found that peanut hearts attracted large flocks of starlings, so we cut them out, because while we have nothing against starlings in moderation, we did not wish to adopt several hundred starlings. When pigeons became a problem, we switched to 100 percent "black oil" sunflower seeds, served only in the feeder, and the pigeons left, commenting mournfully. Those are the only flock birds we have had trouble with. We always have ten or twenty mourning doves around, but that's a manageable number. We draw the line only when birds of any one kind are coming in such numbers that our regular birds are unable to feed.

If squirrels are a problem (we usually put out a little extra for the locals because we have sort of a relationship going now), try hanging your feeder on a very thin, very slack clothesline between two trees or mount a baffle—a sort of wide metal collar that extends out from the feeder pole.

Thickly greasing the feeder pole with petroleum jelly is another effective and inexpensive solution. (A great kid project—messy but useful.) It discourages the squirrels until it wears off, and it is entertaining to watch them leap at the pole with confidence and determination, and slide gracefully back down like reluctant firefighters. They always try again, and they always look as if they can hardly believe this is happening to them. Squirrels are not accustomed to failure.

Melt down a big chunk or two of suet (from the meat department of the supermarket) and then add everything you have on hand while the suet is still liquid: raisins, nuts, oats, cornmeal, seeds, small pieces of apple, whatever. Pour the mixture into empty cottage cheese or yogurt cartons while it is still hot, then set it out on the porch (up high) to cool. When the suet has hardened, pry it out of the mold and put it into a plastic mesh bag that fruit or potatoes came in. Run a bit of yarn or string through the top of the bag and hang it on a tree branch—high. If you hang it too low—say, below six feet—a very hungry, very athletic dog will get it. The birds who find this offering will think they have died and gone to heaven. You will find similar products, but probably not as appetizing as yours, for fairly high prices in the garden shops, so you save a bundle doing it yourself. An adult must be present when the melting of the suet is going on (in a covered pan over low to medium heat) and when things are being stirred into the still-hot suet.

We are approaching the holiday season at the speed of light now, and these bird-feeding extras—"suet puddings" and stuffed pine cones and coconut shells—make good child-to-adult gifts when wrapped in clear or colored food wrap, and finished off with a bow. They are gifts with a future, handmade, and inexpensive, and you can't beat that combination.

You can also use a mesh bag as a hanger for a suet chunk. Take the slab of suet out of its packaging, slip it into the bag, run a piece of yarn or cotton string through the top of the bag, and hang it up. Five minutes, tops. A big piece of suet will last a month or more, and the birds will love it, particularly the woodpeckers.

All through the bird-feeding projects, whenever possible, give the kids a say or something to do. For instance, ask for opinions on where to place the feeder. It should be out in the open, to keep neighborhood cats from creeping up unseen and preying on the birds while they are absorbed in feeding. It should be fairly close to the house so that stocking it in bad weather will not be an ordeal. It should be placed where it can be clearly seen from at least one window, but preferably not from someone's bedroom.

When everything outdoors is white or gray, when the sun doesn't shine for a week at a time, the movement, color, and cheerful music that birds provide become more and more important. The sight of a male cardinal lighting on a bare tree branch against a dead-white sky can restore your spirit for the rest of the day. (It is thought that the increase in the numbers of backyard feeders has been responsible for the way in which birds such as cardinals and mockingbirds have extended their range in the last twenty years. Get with the program!)

Spreading the Good Seed

All around us at this time of year, plant seeds are being eaten, are blowing away or floating downriver, or are latching on to some other means of transportation. Milkweed pods open and clouds of milkweed down rise on every gusty updraft. Underneath each little puff of silk hangs a small brown seed.

Sticktights (spiky little brown weed seed containers) are traveling through the fields and woods on our jeans and our dogs' coats. (Sticktights act exactly like Velcro, carried to the max.) The keys of the maple twirl down the wind, and countless squirrels dart across country roads with fat-husked nuts between their clenched teeth. Everything green that reproduces by seed needs a little help spreading that seed around. Ask the kids what would happen if all seeds just fell where they grew and stayed there. Would that be good or bad? (It would be disastrous. The offspring would come up in a tight little circle around the parent and crowd one another to death or die from lack of sunlight.) So seeds float or hitch or blow away or appeal to collectors who do their part involuntarily. The squirrel's ability to collect and bury nuts for the winter exceeds his ability to remember where he put them, and as a result, forgetful or perhaps merely fickle, squirrels plant platoons of nut trees every year, quite by accident.

You might ask the kids how they think most wild berry seeds are spread. Birds and animals eat the berries for their sweetness and flavor. The berry flesh is utilized during the digestive process, but the seed, protected by a hard coat, is not digested and absorbed. It continues on through the digestive tract and out, and here we go again. The seed is introduced to a brand-new location, and there is even a little soil-enhancer spread around to give it a good start.

One of our best helpers in replanting damaged rain forests is a fruit-eating bat that processes its fruit dinner and discharges the end products (the seeds) in twenty minutes, while it is still flying. The result is that it spreads native fruit seeds aerially while it is still in those areas where they are most likely to flourish. You could learn to love a bat like that.

Why not organize a seed scavenger hunt with a prize to the child who finds the most seeds—all different kinds, of course. A bag of one thousand pinto beans will not do the trick. And there could also be a small prize to the one with the largest seed (an avocado?) and another to the one who comes up with the smallest seed. We can usually find enough categories in any competition so that no one ends up without some recognition. Who has the funniest-looking seed? Or the prettiest seed? (Get out the magnifying glass.) Or the seed from farthest away? Hint: This one may be discovered on your spice shelf.

Let the hunt begin!

Hypothermia: Head It Off at the Pass!

Any book that urges you to get more in touch with the natural world ought to do what it can to see that you survive the encounter—hence a little discussion about hypothermia and coming back alive from the great outdoors.

Hypothermia sounds like a skin condition, doesn't it? ("My dear, I had to wear gloves all evening. My hypothermia was acting up!") But it isn't a skin condition. Under some very special circumstances it is a lifesaver. More often, under other circumstances, it is a killer. You could define hypothermia as a state in which the body loses more warmth than it can produce, until body temperature drops dangerously. Bodily processes slow down, down, down until, if hypothermia is allowed to continue unchecked, they stop.

BASIC FANNY PACK LIST FOR VERY SMALL CHILDREN
- Bandanna
- Red woolen cap
- Choclate bar
- Flashlight
- Whistle
- Big square of plastic

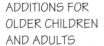

ADDITIONS FOR OLDER CHILDREN AND ADULTS
- Compass
- Large plastic trash bag
- Swiss Army knife
- Weather-proofed matches
- Twenty-foot length of cord

Surgeons use hypothermia to slow metabolic processes while they perform major surgery, usually on the heart. Here it is carefully controlled and saves lives. Outside of the operating room it can happen to anyone who becomes too cold for too long. People have died from hypothermia in every month of the year in this country. Not just mountain climbers but average people who misjudged the weather, or got lost, or pushed on when they should have stopped and taken steps to conserve their remaining energy. People like us.

Hypothermia feels exactly like what it is: a slowing down. Your mind moves more slowly, you can't think. You feel overwhelmed and confused. Your muscles tighten and you become increasingly clumsy and weak. The slower you get, the more chilled you become. And you know where that leads—the ultimate chill.

Anytime you are going for a hike through any spot wilder than a city park, you should take a few small essentials along just in case. There is a list of basics on page 183 organized by the age and abilities of the family member. These things will not save your life under extreme conditions, but they might make the difference if you got lost on a Sunday afternoon hike and the weather closed down on you.

Some basic lost-in-the-woods tips:

First, tell someone at home where you're headed and when you'll be back. That's essential. How are they going to know where to look if you never told them? Also, listen to the weather report. It's one thing to watch a sudden storm beat at the trees in your yard from indoors and quite another to be out there in the storm taking the beating yourself.

Second, when the thought first hits you that you might be lost, STOP. Right then. Make your next thought a reassuring one. Your state of mind is important, and sooner or later if you don't get out of the woods, someone is going to come in and find you, so take it easy. Calmly look around and study the lay of the land. Can you figure your direction from the path of the sun? How about important landmarks you noticed earlier—striking rock formations or a mountain top? Do you hear sounds that might be a clue, such as the rushing of a creek? Did you walk along a creek coming in? Were you walking upstream or downstream? If there are no landmarks to go by, no familiar sounds, and everything looks the same to you in all directions, it's time to explore.

Third, mark your present spot unmistakably in a highly visible way; a bright red bandanna tied to a tree is good. Use that bandanna as the hub of an exploratory wheel, and breaking small branches and overturning rocks as you go as additional insurance against getting lost, strike out in short, straight lines in every likely direction. Out and back like spokes in a wheel. Out and back. Never lose sight of that bandanna. Chances are that if you stopped as soon as you sensed you were lost, you will find the trail or a landmark you can depend on before you have exhausted all the spokes of the wheel.

Fourth, try blowing your whistle (see list). Don't go at it nonstop. Blow three blasts, a sort of universal signal for "Help!" Then stop. If someone is shouting or blowing back at you, you want to be able to hear them. Blow and rest. Blow and rest. A whistle carries farther in the woods and consumes less of your energy than shouting.

Fifth, if there is no response, stop before you exhaust yourself. Get set to be as comfortable and warm as possible while you wait it out. Someone will find you. Your job is to stay calm and stay put and conserve your strength and body heat.

Water conducts heat 240 times more effectively than still air does. (Remember how you felt the last time you climbed out of a warm shower into a cool bathroom, which was probably at least 68 degrees?) If you're lost and the temperature is dropping and it's raining or threatening to rain, do whatever you can to stay dry. Trees, particularly dense evergreens, or overhanging rocks will help a lot. Your wool sweater will be worth its weight in gold stocks right now, because wool wicks moisture away from the body and is, in my opinion, the warmest, most comfortable thing you can have next to you when it's cold and wet. Wear your wool garment next to the skin. Pile the other things you brought over the wool for extra layers of still air insulation.

If it isn't raining but the wind is rising, find a sheltered spot where the wind can't get to you. If there is more than one of you, cuddle up close. If you're alone, scrunch down. Remember the windchill factor? If the wind is still and the temperature is 50 degrees, all you have to deal with is 50 degrees; however, if the temperature holds at 50 degrees but the wind blows at twenty miles per hour, your body is now struggling to stay warm at a windchill factor of 32 degrees, or freezing. Moving air cools a body much more rapidly than still air. Suppose the temperature drops to 40 and wind stays at twenty miles per hour, you'll find yourself up against a windchill factor of 18 degrees, which is very cold indeed if all you're wearing is a shirt and a pair of blue jeans.

Once you have picked your sheltered spot, you probably should build a fire—not just because it will warm you and comfort you but because it or its smoke might be seen by someone else. One of the items on the basics list for adults is waterproofed matches. Find some birch bark still on the tree or a handful of dead twigs on standing timber (when your life is at stake, you are permitted to bend the park rules), add any little scraps of dry paper you might have in your pockets, and start your fire. (I am assuming you carefully cleared the ground of litter before you started this fire.) Lay some small, dry bits of branch beside you before you put match to tinder. Add fuel a little at a time until your fire is well established. If night is coming on soon, gather all the wood you can during what's left of daylight. But never, never go out of sight of your red bandanna while you're collecting wood or tinder.

Now curl up, eat your chocolate bars (see list), and stay put.

If you brought a plastic tarp or poncho, put it over you or under you, whichever will keep you drier and warmer. And above all, remember that people will be pouring into those woods soon, looking for you.

To outfit the kids for hiking, start by allowing everyone to pick his or her own fanny pack. This will be their own pack, which they will wear every time they go into the woods.

For a small child you will need an inexpensive whistle on a cord, a red bandanna (the youngest kids should be told just to tie it to the nearest tree so they'll be easier to find when they're lying down to rest or stay warm; they are too young to be asked to explore the spokes of their location wheel), a rectangle of heavy-duty plastic that he or she can lie on or under for dryness or warmth, a bright red wool cap, and a disposable flashlight.

Explain to the child that if he or she feels cold all over, putting his or her cap on will help all over. We lose a tremendous amount of body heat through our scalps, and the cap will slow that down.

Tuck a chocolate bar into the pack for spring, fall, or winter hikes, and for summer hikes a foil-lined carton of real fruit juice (not one of those "drinks" or "ades" that has so much sugar in them; it will just make the child thirstier). Make it clear that the chocolate is for emergency use, and a sudden craving for chocolate five minutes after leaving camp does not constitute an emergency. (Perhaps letting the child eat the bar on the way home after each hike will ensure compliance on this.)

As they get older, the children may be entrusted with compasses if they know how to use them; the largest size heavy-duty plastic trash bags with head-holes cut in the sealed ends, (to wear over everything like a poncho in case of rain or wind); a Swiss Army knife—the simplest ones are fine; and a length of light cord. If you think they understand how to build a fire safely, give them each a package of waterproofed matches. All these, by the way, are in addition to the basic bandanna, cap, chocolate, flashlight, and whistle kit. Bigger fannies, bigger fanny packs.

The adults in the family will probably carry a small first-aid kit; a topographical map of the area if one is available; and extras such as warm, dry socks, a canteen of water, insect repellent, and a bag of trail mix—a nourishing mix of grains, dried fruits, and nuts that will keep you going for a long time. If there is room, your backpack might include a couple of those "space age" blankets that fold up to fit in a pocket and, unfolded, reflect your own body heat back to you.

If this sounds like a lot of protection, a lot of imagining dire circumstances, I can only say that once you have been lost in the woods, however briefly, as I have, it feels just about right. Most of the purchases will be quite inexpensive and one-time investments.

The Pleiades—Seven Sisters

*I*f the evening is balmy—and once in a while in November you do get a balmy evening—why not take the little nippers out to meet the Seven Sisters, the Pleiades (pronounced plea-ah-dees)? The Pleiades form a tightly knit little cluster of stars. They are so distinctive that once you have found them, you will be able to pick them out immediately on subsequent stargazing expeditions. The Sisters are at their best on very clear nights.

Look to the eastern sky. Go up about one third of the way from the horizon line. You should see at least five stars so close together that it's hard to count them separately. On good nights you will be able to pick out six. If you think you've located the cluster but the individual stars are annoyingly indistinct, try looking just to one side or the other and letting your eyes sort of glide over the Sisters. Don't concentrate intensely and stare directly at them, trying to penetrate the light-years of space between us by sheer willpower. That never seems to work.

Sometimes the Pleiades look as if they are part of a small misty cloud, and that is not far from the truth. If you train a pair of 7 × 50 binoculars on them, you will see lots of other surprisingly bright stars around them—a cloud of stars.

In mythology the Pleiades were the daughters of Atlas, and Orion, the hunter, whom we will meet in December, was chasing them. They were put up in the stars to keep them safe. One of them, the Lost Pleiad (the seventh sister), is rarely seen with the naked eye. She is supposed to be hiding, from sorrow or from shame.

There is a lovely star, Aldebaran, that is quite close to the Pleiades. Come down a little closer to the horizon and you should see an orange star, very bright star. Aldebaran is thirty-six times the diameter of our sun, and fifty-five light-years away. It and the Pleiades are considered part of the Bull, which could be quite confusing to a small child. After all, we talk about these Seven Sisters, but we can really see only six most nights, and then, just when he has that straight, we say, "By the way, these Sisters are part of a Bull." I don't think so. It would destroy our credibility. Just point out Aldebaran and let it ride.

December

Hibernation: A Near Death Experience

*H*ibernation is sometimes referred to as the Big Sleep, but it isn't really just a long sleep. If the hibernating animal's bodily processes continued to function at near normal "sleeping" rates, it would use up all its resources long before winter ended and starve in its sleep. The heartbeat and breathing of animals in deep hibernation slow down almost to the vanishing point. Tests have shown that a hibernating woodchuck's heart may beat only five times a minute. The thirteen-lined squirrel's heart may slow down to that point, and it may breathe only once or twice in a minute or even less.

Take out your watch with the sweep-second hand and count off five periods of twelve seconds each for the kids so they will have some understanding of just how slow those pulse rates are. Twelve seconds is a long time to a child. Then let them count their own pulse rates. (Tips of the index and second fingers should lightly rest on that throbbing place on the inside of the wrist or to one side of the windpipe about halfway down the throat.) Have the child silently count pulse beats while you monitor the watch. Stop at six seconds and multiply the child's figure by ten. That figure will be the child's pulse rate. Ask the child if he or she can go a whole minute without breathing. It's hard.

The body temperature of these animals drops to a point just above that of the surrounding air, perhaps only slightly above freezing. Considering how chilled the woodchuck's body is, it's almost incredible that his blood continues to flow at all if it is being pumped only once every twelve seconds. It must be like cold sludge, moving almost imperceptibly through his veins.

Do the kids know that many bats hibernate? They collect in large colonies and hang from the roofs of caves. They become so stiff and cold that they appear to be already dead, but if you handle them long enough or introduce heat, light, or noise into the cave, you will find that there is plenty of life in the old bats yet. As soon as you leave, which probably won't take long, they will cruise around for a minute, stretching their legs as it were, and then hang it up again.

Bats have to find and take advantage of a ready-made cave. This makes them much more vulnerable than those animals that dig out a den or burrow in a site of their own choosing. If the entrance to the bat cave is just a little too large and too much cold air gets in, the temperature in the cave will fall below freezing and the hibernating bats will never wake up. If for some reason the cave becomes too warm, the rate of the bats' metabolism may increase to the point where they use up their body fat too rapidly and starve. It's not easy being a bat, and the Big Sleep is fraught with peril.

Wilder Candy

Years ago, as we read our way through all the Laura Ingalls Wilder books beginning with *Little House on the Prairie,* we were intrigued by references to a sweet treat that frontier children like Laura and Mary Wilder loved. The book simply said they boiled molasses and sugar together, and poured the mixture onto fresh snow. We decided to try it. After some interesting experiments—all of which were eaten anyway—we arrived at our own version of Wilder candy.

Stir a half cup of dark molasses and a generous cup of granulated sugar together in a pot. Bring the mixture to a boil over medium-high heat, stirring constantly. Continue to boil over medium to medium-high heat for eight to ten minutes, and pour out onto a big pan or cookie sheet heaped with fresh snow. This candy will be sort of molasses taffy. If you boil the mixture five minutes longer—a total of fifteen minutes—and then pour it onto the snow, you should have a molasses brittle.

It is a lot of fun to dribble the candy mixture onto the snow in lacy patterns or figure eights or initials. All the kids should have a chance to dribble, under close adult supervision, using a large spoon or ladle. The initial cooking and stirring is really an adult job. This hot, sugary mixture can burn if it spills, because it clings to the skin and holds its heat.

It's a toss-up which is nicer, the taffy or the brittle. The kids

seem to prefer the taffy, but if you have a lot of big, old fillings, I'd advise you to stick to the brittle. Store any uneaten candy in the freezer on its snow base.

I think it might add to their appreciation of this project if the kids understood that in the 1870s when families like the Wilders lived alone in a clearing in the wilderness, sweet treats were hard to come by. There was little money for anything that wasn't a necessity. Even plain molasses and sugar were special if a family lived a bare-bones existence. When you're bringing in pans of fresh snow and the kids are making patterns on the snow with their ladles of hot syrup, you are reenacting something that children loved to do more than a hundred years ago.

The Wilder books give an authentic picture of the family's experiences, and they are gripping in the way that a vividly told truth is always gripping. You will notice, in these books, that the wilderness and everything it contained was an adversary then—something to be conquered and bent to the family's use if possible. If the wilderness "won" (if wild animals destroyed a crop or preyed on the family cow, if a blizzard swept down unexpectedly before the man of the house could make it safely back to shelter), the family lost, which in some cases meant "died." When you remember that this attitude was prevalent and understandable in many cases (which is not to excuse the same attitude when it was held by people living in thoroughly civilized areas who slaughtered buffalo by the hundreds and thousands for sport) only one hundred years ago, it is easy to understand why conservationists have their work cut out for them today. It takes time to bring about a complete reversal of national attitude.

It Feels Cold, and We Adjust

*C*old weather in November and December seems much more penetrating, more instantly unpleasant, than the same low temperatures do in February or March. Forty-three degrees with a little wind or rain in November can make you feel like going straight home and not coming out again until June. Forty-three degrees with a little breeze or a shower in March can feel like a spring day; you run out for the mail without bothering to put on your jacket. You've adjusted slowly—could we say by degrees?—without even being aware of it.

When you are exposed to cold, the first organ of the body to react is your skin. (Yes, the skin is considered an organ. Our largest organ.) Cold receptors in your skin go into a real frenzy immediately, sending out warning impulses. Blood vessels in the skin constrict, which keeps more blood, good warm blood, in the core of the body where the vital organs are. The hypothalamus, which acts as the body's thermostat, alerts the sympathetic nervous system, which causes the heart to beat faster and triggers an increase in the production of adrenaline. Other stimulating hormones are also released. And the most obvious result of this activity is an uncoordinated, involuntary action by the skeletal muscles, which we call shivering. This whole complicated chain reaction can take place in moments without any conscious effort on our part. It is a beautifully designed survival technique.

Shivering is not just an uncomfortable reaction to cold, it is a response; it accomplishes something. Light shivering increases the amount of warmth produced in the body by 20 percent to 25 percent. Violent shivering can increase heat production by as much as 400 percent. Shivering cannot replace body heat already lost, but it may prevent or at least slow down further loss. Severe shivering is very uncomfortable and like pain, is a highly effective mechanism. Sharp pain and violent shivering cause us to single-mindedly seek relief. They are impossible to ignore, whereas their underlying causes might be ignored if we were totally absorbed in something else.

There is some evidence that people who are determined not to become cold or who are predisposed to enjoy being out in the cold actually do feel it less and are slower to shiver. Mind over matter.

If exposure continues, you may experience frostbite. The first sign is whitening of the affected skin. The best treatment is a gentle bathing of the affected skin with blood-temperature water (test it on the inside of your wrist). Rubbing is out. What you may not realize is that once frostbitten, twice vulnerable. If you have had frostbitten toes before, protect them conscientiously now because the next time they'll succumb more easily and more rapidly. Feet, being way off in left field, circulatorily speaking, are a real problem for some people in cold weather. If we had short, stumpy legs—hippopotamus legs—we might have other problems, but poor circulation in our feet would probably not be one of them.

To observe the speed with which your body and mind respond to temperature changes, try the following experiment, or better yet, have the kids try it. Fill a pail or bowl with hot water, only as hot as can be comfortably tolerated for a short time. Fill another pail or bowl with ice water. Put a third container, filled with lukewarm water, between them. Have one of the kids stick one hand in the hot water and the other in the ice water for fifteen seconds. Then ask him or her to put both hands into the lukewarm water. To the hand that was in the hot water, lukewarm will feel refreshingly cool. To the hand that was submerged in ice water, lukewarm will feel blessedly warm, almost hot. There they are: two hands attached to the same person, about an inch apart in the same water, giving different feedback to their owner's brain. In just fifteen seconds the skin on both hands had started to adjust to the different temperatures. As a species we really are a magnificent piece of work.

If You Plant It, They Will Come

While the yard is stripped down to its bones by winter and the memories of what gave you the most pleasure in the garden last summer are still fresh, why not take a walk around the lot with the kids and talk about your garden of the future? It's possible to create a tiny nature preserve in a very small space. There are dozens of ways by which you can turn an ordinary yard into an oasis for birds and small animals. In a relatively short time there will be more going on outdoors than there is indoors. It doesn't take much money, it just takes a little planning. And right now, with a bare canvas laid out in front of you, is a good time to start. Plan in December, send for the catalogues in January, and order your seeds and plants in February.

First of all, think variety. If your plot is baked in sunshine all day long, you'll need to plant something that throws shade—shrubs, perhaps, and a fast-growing tree or two. If your lot is heavily wooded, you'll have to open it up and let some sunshine in. Take down or radically prune a tree, preferably one that is already showing signs of age. I know this is painful to contemplate, but the results will justify the trauma.

Decide what you want to attract. Every plant on your property should provide something attractive for your favorite birds, animals, or butterflies. For instance, monarch butterflies are among my favorites, and monarchs require—absolutely require—milkweed plants to complete their life cycle, so on this property we encourage milkweed to come early and stay late. It is not a weed any longer to us. Hummingbirds, those little jewels of summer, love trumpet vines, so I have started our own trumpet vine in a sunny corner. White Swan Seed Company (ask at your local garden stores) offers a collection of flower seeds designed specifically to appeal to hummingbirds.

Everyone in the family will have a favorite bird, butterfly, or small animal they'd like to see more of, and the odds are that what attracts one will attract some of the others as well. Search through your wildlife guides for plant preferences and use these plants wherever possible.

Fresh, clear water is always attractive to the birds in summer. Perhaps you could incorporate a bird bath in the garden. We use a big (eighteen inches across) clay-colored plastic saucer about two inches deep for a bird bath. It sits on a big flat rock in the shade of one of the apple trees. The total cost was about three dollars. It works just fine.

If your setup permits, you might leave a small area of your property as is, allowing native wildflowers (what some call weeds) to flourish. Or you could turn the soil in early spring and plant a wildflower seed mixture, which you can find at the garden shops. Over a period of time orchard grass or witch grass may crowd out some of the wildflowers. You may want to reseed about once very five years. But many wildflowers are tough enough to hold their own and even spread in spite of wild grasses, drought, and flood, and they will attract a lovely diversity of birds and butterflies.

In summary, think sunlight and shade; have a family discussion about who you want to attract; do some detective work about what will attract your favorites; then give your small wild customers what they want. If you plant it, they will come.

Refuge from the Storm

While you're planning your backyard nature preserve, leave a little space for a "rustic corner." That's a brush pile in disguise; some neighborhoods will embrace a rustic corner but would discourage any talk of brush piles. That may be why no one builds a good brush pile anymore. The minute a couple of big branches and a bushel basketful of twigs get together, someone comes along and sends it all out with the trash or burns it. What a waste! There is absolutely nothing like a good, big brush pile to increase the appeal of your property for birds and small animals. If you live on a small suburban lot and must be concerned about appearances, read on. We have our little ways. And this project is worth your consideration.

In the winter our brush pile provides absolutely safe nighttime shelter for dozens of birds. No predator is likely to surprise and catch them while they rest in the heart of the pile. Our cat walks past muttering and twitching his tail in frustration. The snow forms a netted quilt over the pile, and the wind cannot penetrate to its center.

In the spring and summer it becomes one big layer-upon-layer nursery. When we walk by, we are scolded by parent birds of a half-dozen species. The earnest piping of hungry nestlings can be heard all day long. The air traffic over the pile is heavier than Thanksgiving weekend at Kennedy Airport. At ground level, rabbits, chipmunks, toads, and very probably deer mice venture out early and late.

In the fall the pile is relatively quiet. It still serves as a refuge for any small creature pursued by hawk or cat, but after the cheerful babble of spring and summer, it seems almost deserted —until the wind turns sharp and snow falls.

If you have a little space to spare (not up against the house where it might pose a fire hazard) and would like to create a powerful natural attraction, start your own small brush pile. A discarded Christmas tree can become a cornerstone of the pile, and after that, all storm debris and pruning remnants will help to broaden its base. Add whatever tough, woody things come to hand, and when volunteers such as elderberry bushes and bittersweet vines begin to spring up in the center of the pile, cheer them on. We're building a tiny fortress here and need all the help we can get.

If you would like to keep your brush pile green most of the year, consider a brier patch (remember Brer Rabbit?), only make it a "bramble" patch. Plant a goodly number of hardy raspberries and blackberries, and let them flourish. Select both trailing and upright varieties so you get height and breadth for your shelter. You'll harvest some fruit—not nearly as much as if you pruned the vines rigorously every year—but enough. You'll also get baby brambles springing up here, there, and elsewhere. Be ruthless: Pull them out with tough gloves on your hands. Try to find a pair of those specially treated woodstove gloves at your stove shop or hardware store. They provide excellent protection for dozens of jobs.

If even a tangle of brambles is too rustic for your neighborhood, send off for three or five old-fashioned hardy roses, old shrub roses that are tough as nails, almost totally carefree, and the talk of the block when they bloom. Pick the largest ones you can find in the catalogues. You'll find ads for the companies that carry the old roses in gardening magazines, and a few good books are available on old roses. Choose some of the upright type and one or two of the rambling or trailing varieties. Plant them fairly close together. You will have to give them the normal first-year care, of course, seeing to it that they are well watered, weed free, and protected from the kid with the lawn mower, but after that they can pretty well fend for themselves and are absolutely beautiful in bloom. It is puzzling why more people don't grow them.

If thorny things are not your bag (thorns are a small creature's best friend sometimes), how about a thicket of forsythia? Plant a half-dozen small forsythia shrubs fairly close together, care for them tenderly until they are established, and then leave them alone. No pruning or shaping into stiff little balls. They will create a big safe zone for lots of wildlife in time. If there is an old fruit tree on your property, preferably one that no longer throws dense shade, plant your shrubs around its base. It will provide the ultimate in protection at the core of the thicket.

Never refer to your brambles as a brier patch or your forsythia as a green brush pile; use socially acceptable terms. If your neighbor remarks that your forsythia is taking over the south side of your house (this man should get a life; doesn't

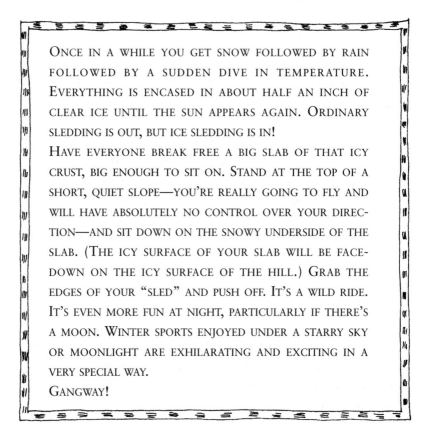

ONCE IN A WHILE YOU GET SNOW FOLLOWED BY RAIN FOLLOWED BY A SUDDEN DIVE IN TEMPERATURE. EVERYTHING IS ENCASED IN ABOUT HALF AN INCH OF CLEAR ICE UNTIL THE SUN APPEARS AGAIN. ORDINARY SLEDDING IS OUT, BUT ICE SLEDDING IS IN!

HAVE EVERYONE BREAK FREE A BIG SLAB OF THAT ICY CRUST, BIG ENOUGH TO SIT ON. STAND AT THE TOP OF A SHORT, QUIET SLOPE—YOU'RE REALLY GOING TO FLY AND WILL HAVE ABSOLUTELY NO CONTROL OVER YOUR DIRECTION—AND SIT DOWN ON THE SNOWY UNDERSIDE OF THE SLAB. (THE ICY SURFACE OF YOUR SLAB WILL BE FACE-DOWN ON THE ICY SURFACE OF THE HILL.) GRAB THE EDGES OF YOUR "SLED" AND PUSH OFF. IT'S A WILD RIDE. IT'S EVEN MORE FUN AT NIGHT, PARTICULARLY IF THERE'S A MOON. WINTER SPORTS ENJOYED UNDER A STARRY SKY OR MOONLIGHT ARE EXHILARATING AND EXCITING IN A VERY SPECIAL WAY.

GANGWAY!

he have anything better to worry about?), stand tall, snap your suspenders, and say, "Yes. Eileen and I never dreamed that someday we would have a stand of forsythia like that." *Stand* is an impressive word. Be seen on a spring holiday morning taking pictures of the kids in front of the forsythia in full holiday regalia. If this same pest refers to your brambles in uncomplimentary terms, say, "They are doing well, aren't they? I always say it pays to buy the best." Don't try to convert him. Just refuse to accept his idea of what's right for you and yours.

What Did I Do to Deserve a Charge Like This?

*I*t's probably already happened to you for the first time this season. You slide across a car seat, reach for the handle, and *snap!*—static electricity strikes again. You shuffle across the rug, only about half-awake, start to open the front door to get the morning paper, and *zing*! The shock you get from the doorknob is enough to make your eyes water. It's too early in the morning for pain like that, and as often as it happens, you never get used to it.

How does it happen? We have to start at square one, the atom. The atom's center is a positively charged nucleus. There are negatively charged electrons swinging around the nucleus in orbit. Some of these negatively charged electrons wouldn't leave home for any amount of money, but others might, if someone made them an offer.

Human beings are almost always carrying an electrical charge, either slightly negative or slightly positive. When, through friction (such as brushing, rubbing, or shuffling) we make an offer, we pick up those fickle negative electrons and acquire a strong negative charge. As we approach the metal doorknob, which is normally uncharged, or neutral, the excess of negative electrons on our hands repels the negative electrons on the surface of the doorknob (or, more properly, the part of the knob closest to our hand), and it becomes in part positive. This opposite charge is called an "image charge."

Negative electrons on the knob flee from our approaching negative hand, and negative electrons in the air between your hand and the knob are repelled by the charge in your hand and rush toward the positive area on the knob. In their haste they hit nitrogen atoms in the air, ionizing them and releasing two or more electrons every time, which in turn join the stampede and hit other nitrogen atoms, which release more electrons, and so on, until we get what is called an "avalanche" effect of negative electrons all rushing hellbent toward that positive part of the knob. There aren't very many free electrons in the air until this ionization gets going. Eventually there is enough of them to create a path of ionized atoms, which is actually like a thin wire connecting your hand and the knob, and at that point, current can flow, and does, through the electrical field, giving your hand one hell of a shock.

It's not just your imagination that it really hurts. Although brief, it is a strong charge.

Why winter? Why does this happen most often when the weather is cold and dry?

The air is much drier in winter, and dry air is an effective insulator. In summer there are many more water molecules present in the air. They conduct electricity quite well, much more easily than the dry air. When that charged electrical field between your hand and the knob starts to build up, a good deal of the charge leaks or escapes into or through water molecules. If a current does pass between you and the knob, it is so slight that you do not feel it.

It may occur to you that it would take an extremely slow hand moving at a snail's pace toward that knob to allow time for all this ionizing and charging to take place, and doubt may be entering your mind. Actually the whole process (like so many we live with every day but are unaware of) takes place in a fraction of a second.

The kids can see this negative to positive movement in action whenever they brush or comb their freshly washed and dried hair. On a cold, clear day, fine hair will follow a charged comb right up into the air for a second or two. The charge was built up during the brushing and combing. A comb, once it is negatively charged, will pick up small pieces of paper or a down feather, and hold it until those electrons have jumped ship again. If placed close to the pointed end of a compass needle, a charged comb or brush will cause the needle to temporarily abandon true north and swing to the east or west. This is called an electrostatic effect. If one of the children has long hair and is wearing a wool sweater, take her into a darkened room with a mirror and have her comb or brush her hair vigorously down over her shoulders. Wherever the ends of her hair meet the sweater, sparks will happen. It will look as if a small squadron of fireflies has landed on her shoulders.

Orion, Mighty Hunter

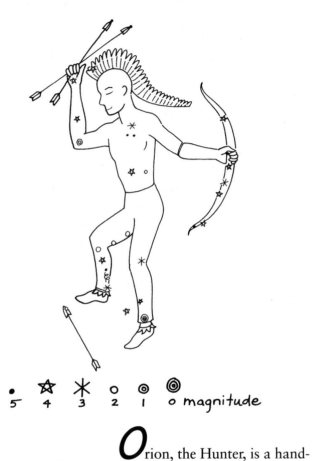

• ☆ ✳ ○ ◎ ◉
5 4 3 2 1 0 magnitude

Orion, the Hunter, is a handsome constellation. You can't miss him this month if the eastern sky is clear. He will be stretched out low over the eastern horizon early in the evening.

Start by looking for his "belt"—three bright stars in a straight line. If you extend your arm, the widest part of your thumb will just fit between the stars on either end of the belt. In our drawing, Orion has become a Native American youngster and his belt now marks his left thigh.

Next look for Betelgeuse, twinkling like an amber jewel above and to the left of Orion's belt, and Rigel, brilliant, blue-white star, below and to the right of his belt. Betelgeuse marks Orion's left elbow (from our vantage point) and Rigel marks his right ankle. Now you should be able to pick out his other foot, the arrows he holds in front of him to his left, his left calf, and the bow he holds out behind and above him.

Halfway down what would be Orion's left calf, you may see a pale blur. This is the Great Orion Nebula, a luminous gas cloud. Although it may look like a small, indistinct star to us, it is widespread beyond our comprehension. Three hundred light-years of distance renders it almost invisible to us on earth.

Orion's three stars in a row and Betelgeuse are so distinctive that they will draw your eye to the Hunter from now on, no matter where in the sky he happens to be.

Suggested Further Reading for Each Month

January

Bull, John, and Farrand, Jr., John. *Audubon Society Field Guide to North American Birds.* New York: Alfred A. Knopf, 1977.

Lopez, Barry. *Of Wolves and Men.* New York: Charles Scribner's Sons, 1978.

Martin, A. G. *Hand Taming Wild Birds at the Feeder.* Brattleboro, VT: Alan C. Hood and Co., 1990.

Old Farmer's Almanac, The. Dublin, NH: Yankee Publishing, 1992 ed. (Published annually).

Rey, H. A. *The Stars.* Boston, MA: Houghton Mifflin Co., 1980.

Stokes, Donald and Lillian. *A Guide to Animal Tracking and Behavior.* Boston, MA: Little, Brown and Co., 1987.

Williams, W. *Birds of the Northeast.* Tampa, FL: World Publications, 1989.

Wolpert, Tom, and Stevens, Gareth. *Wolves, Wolf Magic for Kids.* NorthWord Press, 1990.

February

Ingram, Jay. *The Science of Everyday Life.* New York: Viking Penguin, 1989.

Mann, Richard E. *Backyard Sugarin'.* Woodstock, VT: Countryman Press, 1992.

Schaefer, Vincent J., and Day, John A. *A Field Guide to the Atmosphere.* Boston, MA: Houghton Mifflin Co., 1981.

Serrao, John. *Nature's Events.* Harrisburg, PA: Stackpole Books, 1992.

March

Dickerson, Mary. *The Frog Book.* New York: Dover Publications, 1969.

Forrester, Frank H. *1001 Questions Answered About the Weather*. New York: Dover Publications, 1981.

Keen, Richard. *Skywatch East*. Golden, CO: Fulcrum Publishing, 1992.

Schaefer, Vincent J., and Day, John A. *A Field Guide to the Atmosphere*. Boston, MA: Houghton Mifflin Co., 1981.

Walpole, Brenda. *175 Science Experiments to Amuse and Amaze Your Friends*. New York: Random House, 1988.

April

Harlow, William M. *Trees of the Eastern and Central United States and Canada*. New York: Dover Publications, 1957.

Keen, Richard. *Skywatch East*. Golden, CO: Fulcrum Publishing, 1992.

Rey, H. A. *The Stars*. Boston, MA: Houghton Mifflin Co., 1980.

Serrao, John. *Nature's Events*. Harrisburg, PA: Stackpole Books, 1992.

Walker, Bryce. *Earthquake*. Alexandria, VA: Time-Life Books, 1982.

Watson, Lyall. *The Water Planet*. New York: Crown Publications, 1988.

Williams, Jack. *The Weather Book*. New York: Vintage Books, 1992.

May

Dickerson, Mary. *The Frog Book*. New York: Dover Publications, 1969.

Hubbell, Sue. *A Country Year*. New York: Random House, 1986.

Ingram, Jay. *The Science of Everyday Life*. New York: Viking Penguin, 1989.

Simon, Seymour. *Pets in a Jar*. New York: Puffin Books, 1979.

June

Allison, Linda. *The Sierra Club Summer Book*. New York: Charles Scribner's Sons, 1977.

Keen, Richard. *Skywatch East*. Golden, CO: Fulcrum Publishing, 1992.

Kopper, Philip. *The Wild Edge*. Chester, CT: Globe Pequot Press, 1991.

Rey, H. A. *The Stars*. Boston, MA: Houghton Mifflin Co., 1980.

Williams, Jack. *The Weather Book*. New York: Vintage Books, 1992.

July

Forrester, Frank H. *1001 Questions Answered About the Weather*. New York: Dover Publications, 1981.

Keen, Richard. *Skywatch East*. Golden, CO: Fulcrum Publishing, 1992.

Rey, H. A. *The Stars*. Boston, MA: Houghton Mifflin Co., 1980.

Schaefer, Vincent J., and Day, John A. *A Field Guide to the Atmosphere*. Boston, MA: Houghton Mifflin Co., 1981.

Simon, Seymour. *Pets in a Jar*. New York: Puffin Books, 1979.

Thomas, Dian. *Roughing It Easy*. Provo, UT: Brigham Young University Press, 1975.

Thomas, Dian. *Roughing It Easy 2*. New York: Warner Books, 1978.

August

Rey, H. A. *The Stars*. Boston, MA: Houghton Mifflin Co., 1980.

Serrao, John. *Nature's Events*. Harrisburg, PA: Stackpole Books, 1992.

September

Hoffman, Don. *Wanderer, the Monarch Butterfly*. Morro Bay, CA: Morro Bay State Park Museum, 1989.

Keen, Richard. *Skywatch East*. Golden, CO: Fulcrum Publishing, 1992.

Rey, H. A. *The Stars*. Boston, MA: Houghton Mifflin Co., 1980.

Schaefer, Vincent J., and Day, John A. *A Field Guide to the Atmosphere*. Boston, MA: Houghton Mifflin Co., 1981.

October

Harlow, W. M. *Trees of the Eastern and Central United States and Canada*. New York: Dover Publications, 1957.

Koch, Maryjo. *Bird, Egg, Feather, Nest*. New York: Stewart, Tabori & Chang, 1992.

Serrao, John. *Nature's Events*. Harrisburg, PA: Stackpole Books, 1992.

Watts, May T., and Watts, Tom. *Winter Tree Finder*. Berkeley, CA: Nature Study Guild, 1970.

November

Angier, Bradford. *How to Stay Alive in the Woods*. New York: Collier Books, 1984.

Manning, Harvey. *Backpacking, One Step at a Time*. New York: Vintage Books, 1986.

Rey, H. A. *The Stars*. Boston, MA: Houghton Mifflin Co., 1980.

Whitefeather, Willy. *Willy Whitefeather's Outdoor Survival Handbook for Kids*. Tucson, AZ: Harbinger House, 1990.

December

Allison, Linda. *The Wild Inside*. Boston, MA: Little, Brown and Co., 1988.

Curtis, Will. *The Nature of Things*. Woodstock, VT: Countryman Press, 1984.

Rey, H. A. *The Stars*. Boston, MA: Houghton Mifflin Co., 1980.

Wilder, Laura Ingalls. *Little House in the Big Woods*. New York: Harper & Row, 1971.

Index